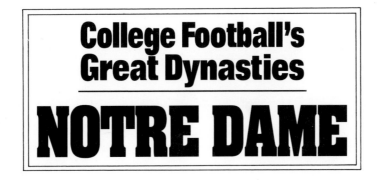

College Football's
Great Dynasties
NOTRE DAME

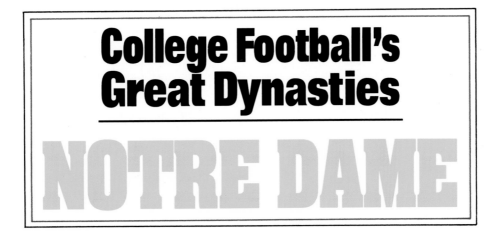

College Football's Great Dynasties

NOTRE DAME

Roland Lazenby

SMITHMARK

Published by Smithmark Publishers
112 Madison Avenue
New York, New York 10016

Produced by
Brompton Books Corp.
15 Sherwood Place
Greenwich, CT 06830

ISBN 0-8317-3477-9

Printed in Hong Kong

10 9 8 7 6 5 4 3 2 1

Page 1: *Coach Frank Leahy gives his 1941 Fighting Irish a preseason chalk talk. Leahy's achievements during his coaching tenure were officially recognized in 1970, when he was inducted into the NFF Hall of Fame.*

Page 2: *Notre Dame Coach Lou Holtz is drenched with icewater by Bryan Flannery after his team pulled off a 21-6 win over the Colorado Buffaloes in the Orange Bowl, 1 January 1990.*

Page 3: *Notre Dame players congratulate each other after a big play. With its legacy of greatness, Notre Dame football inspires a strong sense of team spirit.*

This page: *Notre Dame's legendary Coach Knute Rockne poses with football candidates before practice begins for the 1930 season. Rockne's squad would pull off an undefeated season to win their second consecutive national championship.*

Contents

Introduction

In 1842 a small band of Holy Cross Fathers led by Edward Sorin came from France to South Bend, Indiana, to found a new school for the immigrants who were then pouring into the young state. Only a few years earlier South Bend had been a mere wilderness trading post situated on the Indiana bend of the St. Joseph River, but it had grown so rapidly that it was now both an incorporated town and the county seat. Father Sorin set up his school in an old log building a few miles north of the town and named it, in honor of the Mother of God, Notre Dame.

From such humble beginnings arose one of the world's great universities, one that today boasts colleges of arts and letters, science, law, engineering and commerce and that offers advanced degrees in some 15 departments. It is still owned and operated by the Congregation of Holy Cross of the Roman Catholic Church, and it still adheres to its tradition of opening its doors to students of all faiths. And of course there is one other thing about Notre Dame: on average, it has produced the best college football that this century has witnessed.

Notre Dame did not invent football; the university was in fact something of a latecomer to the game. But when it did finally begin to play in 1887 it embarked on a course that would lead it into the realm of sports legend, and today it has the highest winning percentage in college football

Above: *A member of Notre Dame's marching band contributes her part to school spirit.*

Right: *The Irish halftime show is about to begin during a Notre Dame-Purdue contest. Marching formations and enthusiastic renditions add color and character to Notre Dame's football tradition.*

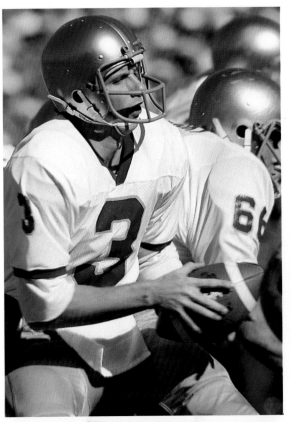

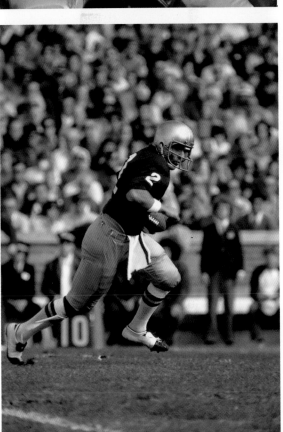

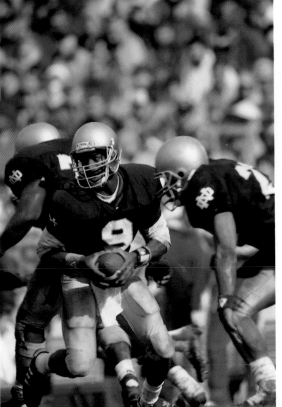

history. To be sure, much of that success came under the stewardship of three great coaches. First there was Knute Rockne, whose lifetime record of 105-12-5 gave him a winning percentage of .881, the highest ever in college *or* pro football. Then, a decade later, there was Frank Leahy, whose Notre Dame career record was an amazing 87-11-9. And finally, a decade after Leahy, came Ara Parseghian, who, in 11 years at Notre Dame ran up an equally astonishing tally of 95-17-4.

Along with legendary coaches, Notre Dame produced legendary players: Gipp, the Four Horsemen, Bertelli, Lujak, Harte, Hornung, Huarte, Theismann, Montana . . . indeed, the roster is too long even to try to reproduce here.

Such a tradition of football excellence inevitably sets high – some might say un-

Above: *The potent backfield combination of 1924 – otherwise known as the Four Horsemen of Notre Dame – wreaked havoc for the Irish on their way to becoming legend.*

realistically high – standards. Gerry Faust, for example, was undeniably a winning coach at 30-26-1, but this record, coupled with the fact that Faust never came close to winning a national championship, was by no means good enough for Notre Dame fans, who considered Faust a failure. They wouldn't settle just for a winning perform-ance; they had come to expect, as though it were their right, a legendary performance. "I can't live up to all the expectations," lamented Lou Holtz when he was named to succeed Faust in 1986. "I look at those records put up by Rockne, Leahy and Par-seghian, and I swear to gosh it's a mis-print."

The intense passions that Notre Dame football generates among students, alumni and fans could easily have produced an ex-treme version of the kind of classroom-*vs*-athletics conflict that has bedevilled so many other universities with outstanding sports programs. Yet with a few minor ex-ceptions, Notre Dame has been remarkably

free of such tensions. No doubt the fact that it is privately owned, is subject to Catholic disciplines and has been well administered has helped to make it resistant to partisan pressures. But equally important is the spirit of the place, a spirit animated by a passion for excellence so pervasive that it could never be satisfied with excellence on the playing field alone. Consider: of the nearly 500 scholarship athletes who, since 1965, remained in school for four years, fewer than 10 failed to graduate. Remark-ing on the fact that in 1986 the school lost only as many students (six) as it did football games, Lou Holtz commented, "Notre Dame is one of the few places that is per-ceived from the outside as being great and is actually even better than that."

Thus when, on home-game Saturdays in Notre Dame Stadium, 59,075 voices rise in the familiar chorus, "Cheer, cheer for old Notre Dame/Wake up the echoes cheering her name," it's not just football they're sing-ing about.

Above left: *Coach Frank Leahy (left) and Assistant Coach Moose Krause watch the 1943 team.*

Above: *Notre Dame cheerleader Joe Gargan had much to cheer about in 1920, as the Irish pulled off their second consecutive unbeaten season.*

Left: *Undefeated in 1930, Notre Dame's legendary Coach Knute Rockne poses with players Frank Carideo and Tom Conley before the team's departure for the season-ending game with Southern Cal.*

1. The Beginning 1887-99

Above: *Notre Dame's founder, Reverend Edward Sorin, pictured in 1905. Father Sorin immigrated from France in 1842 and established the school in South Bend, Indiana.*

Right: *Notre Dame's first football team of 1888 was 1-2-0, with a win over the Harvard School of Chicago and two losses to Michigan.*

Far right: *Father Thomas Walsh, the president of Notre Dame from 1881 to 1893.*

It's fitting that Notre Dame's football history begins with the University of Michigan. Since the two schools met for Notre Dame's first game in November 1887, their football programs have struggled for the position atop the all-time standings of American college football. Michigan has won more games than any other college football team. Notre Dame is second in total victories yet the Irish hold the top spot in the all-time standings by virtue of their winning percentage.

Michigan had been playing football for a decade or so when, in November 1887, its team leaders suggested the Wolverines travel to South Bend to give the Notre Dame boys a lesson in the game. Although the Ivy League, particularly Yale and Walter Camp, ruled over college football in the 1880s, Michigan had begun to establish its football tradition in 1887. The Wolverines fancied themselves "the champions of the West" and showed a readiness to demonstrate their prowess across the region. According to some, the Notre Dame boys were eager to try the new game and agreed to the meeting if their visitors would teach them the rules and demonstrate plays before the competition began.

College football in the 1870s had been played on a long, wide field (140 by 70 yards), which was unmarked save for the goal and midfield stripes. The number of players on a side numbered 15. By the early 1880s the size of the field was decreased to 110 by 53 yards, and the number of players was trimmed to 11 per side. The game's early participants liked to be known for their rakish toughness. They disdained padding as something for sissies and wore instead sweaters or canvas jerseys (and were often called canvasbacks). There was no headgear, so the players grew their hair long to pad their skulls when they smacked heads. The art of tackling was in its rudimentary stages. As a result, the games were often rough affairs of pushing and punching. Noses were broken, teeth knocked out, heads and limbs bruised – all badges of courage to be worn proudly after the game.

A Yale graduate, Walter Camp spent the 1880s overseeing the development of rules of American amateur football. By the time Notre Dame played its first game, the concept of a line of scrimmage had evolved. No longer did action begin with a rugby scrum. It had been established that each team would have three downs to gain five yards for a first down. And to help matters, the

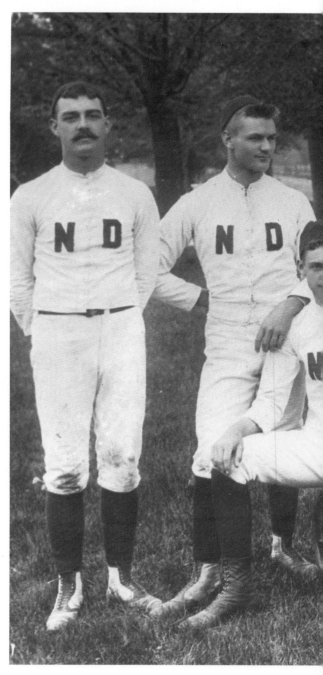

field was marked off with lines every five yards, bringing the concept of gridiron to young college football minds. By that November 1887 the scoring system allowed four points for a touchdown, five for a field goal, two for a point after and two for a safety.

The Wolverines came to South Bend on the Wednesday morning of 23 November. In a nice gesture that has somehow been lost over the decades, a committee of Notre Dame students met the Michigan players and took them on a tour of the campus. With those preliminaries concluded, these young players unceremoniously initiated college football's greatest tradition. First, for demonstration purposes, the teams were divided into two groups, mixing Notre Dame and Michigan players. After some minutes of running practice plays and demonstrating the rules, the schools broke off to their original sides and played what

was termed an "inning" of ball.

Not wanting to seem ungracious guests, the Wolverines ran up a respectable 8-0 score, then retired to the dinner table, where Notre Dame's President Walsh thanked them for the demonstration. The Michigan players still had time to catch the train for Chicago, where they were scheduled to play an Ivy League alumni group the next day.

The event was such a success that the two schools resumed it the following April in a two-game series. Again, the Wolverines traveled to South Bend, where the Notre Dame team had arranged to play the game in Green Stocking Ball Park. Reports have estimated the crowd at more than 400. What they witnessed was a display of Michigan's experience. The Wolverines won, 26-6, sowing more than a bit of irritation in the Irish soul.

The next noon, the Michigan boys came

Above: *Notre Dame players pose for a team photograph with their first coach, James L. Morison, in 1894. The team finished 3-1-1 that year.*

to the campus for a meal and a ride on the lake. Whatever strands of civility that held the afternoon in place were broken later that day on the football field. One of the Michigan players had been injured in the first game, and it was decided that he would trade places with the referee, Edward Sprague, who would then suit up for Michigan. Fired by their humiliation the day before, the Irish lads toughened in the second game. While they hadn't yet figured the intricacies of offense (there were few in the early version of football), the Notre Dame boys put up a fine defense that April afternoon. But another in a string of disputes broke out with about two minutes to play. While the teams argued, Sprague snatched the ball from the referee's hands, and raced for a touchdown. The Notre Dame players argued vociferously and claimed Sprague had stepped out of bounds. The referee, however, allowed the play to stand, and the Wolverines went on to a 10-4 victory.

Notre Dame next played that December, when Harvard School in Chicago came to South Bend for a game. The Irish, captained by Edward Prudhomme, won 20-0, for their first victory. They had hopes of a rematch with Michigan. But the Michigan program had fallen into some disorganiza-tion, and a game couldn't be arranged. Notre Dame finally arranged a match at Northwestern University in November 1889. Again Prudhomme was captain (there was no coach), and again the Irish won, 9-0.

Notre Dame played no intercollegiate football in 1890-91. Then, in 1892, Captain Pat Coady helped reorganize the team with a two-game schedule, both at home. Eager for a rampage, Notre Dame indulged in a common college practice of that era and whipped up on South Bend High School, 56-0, on 19 October. The test that season was to come several weeks later when, just before Thanksgiving, the Irish entertained Hillsdale. That game ended in a 10-10 tie.

The 1893 schedule was ambitious, four games from 25 October to 30 November, then a fifth game on New Year's Day 1894. Played at home, the first four brought Notre Dame a winning streak. In succession, the Irish defeated Kalamazoo 34-0 and Albion 8-6; then, despite a snow-covered field, they trounced DeLaSalle 28-0 and Hillsdale 22-10. The New Year's game at the University of Chicago brought Notre Dame's only loss, 8-0.

For the next season team leaders brought in a former player from Michigan, James L Morison, as the team's first coach. He quickly put together a five-game schedule. His team opened the season on 13 October with a 14-0 home win over Hillsdale. The resulting excitement died a bit when Albion tied the Irish a week later in another home game, 6-6. Nearly a month later Notre Dame defeated Wabash 30-0, and then Rush Medical 18-6. A few days after Thanksgiving, Albion returned for a rematch and whipped Notre Dame 19-12.

After finishing 3-1-1, Morison moved on to coach Hillsdale. He was replaced by H G Hadden in 1895, and Notre Dame finished 3-1 against an interesting collection of club teams – Northwestern Law, Illinois Cycling Club, Indianapolis Artillery and Chicago Physicians and Surgeons. The artillery boys pounded the Irish 18-0.

Frank E Hering had performed his undergraduate work at the University of Chicago, where he played football under the famous Amos Alonzo Stagg. Hering entered Notre Dame to study law and served as player/coach of the football team (intercollegiate rules on undergraduate eligibility had yet to be adopted). Under Hering, the schedule was expanded to seven games for 1896, all of them at home. Hering, a strong student and leader, gained almost immediate popularity, despite opening with two losses, to Chicago Physicians and Surgeons and the University of Chicago.

His first win came against South Bend Commercial Athletic Club, 46-0. After a win over Albion and a loss to Purdue, Hering's edition of the Irish murdered Highland Views 82-0 and edged a semiprofessional team from Beloit, Wisconsin, 8-0 in a cold rain.

Hering brought stability to the team by remaining three seasons as coach. Beyond that, his major accomplishment was an upgrading of the schedule. For 1897 Notre Dame finished 4-1-1 against a slate that included Michigan State, Chicago and DePauw. Hering's biggest coup came in 1898, his last season, with the resumption of the Michigan rivalry, which had been on hold nine seasons since the dispute of 1888. Unfortunately, the Wolverines continued their dominance, 23-0, in Notre Dame's first game at Michigan. The 1898 schedule also included Illinois, Michigan State, Indiana and DePauw. Hering closed out his career at Notre Dame with a 60-0 win over Albion.

The schedule expanded to 10 games in 1899, as James McWeeney took over as coach. The Irish finished 6-3-1 but lost another away game to Michigan, 12-0, leaving another bitter cud to chew over the winter. Notre Dame had yet to gain a win over the Wolverines. But that and much more would come.

Left: *The Irish team was led by player/coach Frank E. Hering in 1896, when their schedule expanded to seven games. Hering played several positions, and his enthusiastic leadership spirited Notre Dame to four victories that year.*

2. The New Century 1900-09

Pat O'Dea, an Australian who had gained fame as the "Kangaroo Kicker" for the University of Wisconsin, coached Notre Dame in 1900-01. His first team finished 6-3-1 but lost to Michigan again. Even worse, O'Dea's alma mater humiliated Notre Dame 54-0 in Madison. Michigan was dropped from the schedule the next season, and Notre Dame opened with a scoreless tie with the South Bend Athletic Club. But from there on the team played well, losing only to Northwestern 2-0 in a heavy rainfall. The team's big victory came over Indiana, 18-5, in the rain.

The one-eyed James F Faragher replaced O'Dea as Notre Dame coach for 1902. An Ohio native, Faragher had played football at West Virginia, Nebraska and Duquesne before coming to Notre Dame in 1900 to participate. Faragher, who had lost his eye in a

Above left: *Frank "Shag" Shaughnessy played Notre Dame football all four years of his college career, becoming team captain his senior year of 1904. Shaughnessy went on to play professional baseball.*

Left: *Louis "Red" Salmon was Notre Dame's first great football hero. The five-foot-ten, 175-pound fullback led the team to its first undefeated season in 1903. He was named to Walter Camp's All-America third team that year.*

football game, had played two seasons for the Irish, then became coach. He was a spirited, enthusiastic teacher of the game. His 1902 team finished 6-2-1, with a loss to Michigan and a tie with Purdue. On 15 November the Irish defeated American Medical 92-0!

Success would grow in the 1903 season, Notre Dame's first undefeated. Led by 175-pound fullback Louis "Red" Salmon, the Irish rang up 292 points over nine games while holding their opponents scoreless. The only blemish was a scoreless tie with Northwestern on 14 November.

Right: *Notre Dame's president, Father John W. Cavanaugh, kept a watchful eye over the football program during the early years of reform.*

Regardless of the schedule, the season brought the first national recognition to South Bend, as team captain Salmon was named to Walter Camp's All-America third team.

Faragher went on to become a campus cop the next season, a post that he would hold for years, and Salmon assumed the coaching duties. His 1904 team finished 5-3, with lopsided losses to Wisconsin, Kansas and Purdue, the only major teams on the schedule. The season highlights included a 107-yard return of a fumbled punt by Frank Shaughnessy against Kansas (the field was 110 yards). "Shag" Shaughnessy went on to a career as a professional baseball player and executive.

In 1905 Notre Dame again whipped a series of club teams and graduate schools, but they lost four games, most of them with other university teams.

College football remained a brutal game, but a change for the better came in 1905 when President Theodore Roosevelt saw a photograph of a bloodied Swarthmore player being carried off the field. Outraged, he demanded that college football clean up its act or face abolition.

The result of the Roosevelt uproar was a White House conference between the President and representatives of the Ivy League's Big Three – Harvard, Princeton and Yale. From there, the football powers of the East agreed to form a rules committee with a goal of taking the game out of the rowdy rut it had fallen into.

The committee met in 1906 and offered several new rules, the most memorable being legalization of the forward pass. The pass had been used irregularly in games for years, and the rules members agreed it was time to make it official. But they also strapped it with enough restrictions to chill its impact. Although the pass would eventually prove its usefulness and catch on at colleges across the country, it was still viewed as a sissified thing. The real contribution the 1906 rules committee made toward lessening the violence in football was the establishment of a 'neutral zone' on the line of scrimmage. Theretofore linemen had battered each other before the ball was snapped, which led to much fighting and slugging. But the neutral zone forbade off-sides contact until the ball was put into play.

In 1910 the rules were further amended to add a fourth offensive down, a factor that increased the use of the pass. (Third down quickly gained recognition as the passing down). The new rules also disallowed line-men lining up in the backfield unless they were positioned five yards behind the line of scrimmage. This eliminated the hurtling, smashing interference that caused so many injuries.

In those seasons of reform Father John Cavanaugh, Notre Dame president, kept a loving, watchful eye on the football pro-gram. Tom Barry, a Brown University alumnus and law school graduate, served as coach for the 1906 and 1907 seasons and produced two fine teams with large lines (averaging better than 210 pounds) and swift, efficient backfields. The '06 team lost only to Indiana, and the only setback for the

'07 unit was a scoreless tie with the Hoosiers, giving Indiana a temporary edge over Michigan as Notre Dame's most in-tense rivalry.

Victor Place, a Dartmouth product, re-placed Barry as coach for 1908, and the Notre Dame success continued. The Irish solved the Indiana riddle 11-0 but lost once again to Michigan in mid-October.

Frank "Shorty" Longman, a University of Michigan man, moved in as Notre Dame coach for 1909 and finally ended the drought against the Wolverines. The Irish beat Michigan 11-3 in Michigan, and when they returned home elated students met them at the train and paraded them through the town. All in all, it was a banner year, as Notre Dame won the first seven games, out-scoring opponents 236-14. Hopes of a perfect season died with the last game, a 25 November meeting with Mar-quette that ended scoreless. Still, regional newspapers bestowed the unofficial "cham-pions of the West" distinction on the Irish.

The next season, a scrawny and un-heralded freshman end, Knute Rockne, would join the team, and the football world would never be the same.

Below: *Coached by Frank "Shorty" Longman, the Fighting Irish finally defeated their Michigan nemesis in 1909 on their way to an undefeated season.*

3. The Young Rockne 1910-17

The legend of Knute Rockne has always loomed over American college football, even through the decades of change since his death in 1931. The son of a Norwegian carriagemaker and engineer, Rockne spent his boyhood in the Logan Square Park area of Chicago. At Chicago's Northwest High School he distinguished himself in track as a pole vaulter and half-miler. He had hopes of attending the University of Illinois, but family money was scarce. Several teammates from the Illinois Athletic Club had

decided to attend Notre Dame, where costs were lower, and they influenced Rockne to do the same. He still needed prep courses to gain admittance, but after passing those the 22-year-old Rockne traveled to South Bend and began life as a freshman in Brownson Hall. His roommate was an energetic 18-year-old Wisconsin native, Gus Dorais. One of college football's great passing combinations had made its first connection.

Dorais would develop into a fine quarter-

back, and the 150-pound Rockne into a crafty end. But before that happened, Notre Dame's legend had to endure his time as a scrub.

He failed in his first tryout with the football team, so Rockne turned his attention back to track, where his speed convinced coach Frank Longman that the little Norwegian might make a football end after all. Meanwhile, Dorais, who had a reputation as a fine baseball pitcher, was also impressing the coach and eventually made the starting lineup.

Against a mild schedule, the 1910 Irish finished 4-1-1, with a loss to Michigan State and a tie with Marquette. Longman left after the season and was replaced by John Marks, a former halfback at Dartmouth. In two years he never lost a game as Notre Dame coach. The Irish scored 222 points in 1911 and gave up only 9, finishing 6-0-2.

With Dorais as captain, Notre Dame opened the 1912 season with a 116-7 win over St Viator. From there a collection of clubs and small colleges fell until a mid-season game at Pittsburgh in the snow, which the Irish only narrowly won, 3-0. At season's end Notre Dame finally ended a three-year streak of tie games with Marquette, slashing past the Warriors 69-0, and finished the school's first unbeaten, untied season at 7-0.

Jess Harper was named Notre Dame football coach and athletic director for the 1913 season. The big excitement of his first year came when Army needed a team to replace Yale on the schedule. To the eastern football establishment Notre Dame was a little-known team out of the Midwest. Eager to prepare, Harper reportedly met many of the Irish players at the train station as they returned to school that fall.

Over the summer Dorais and Rockne had taken jobs at a resort in Cedar Point, Ohio. In their off hours they turned their attention to passing. Dorais had been working to perfect a spiral with his throwing. As the story goes, that summer at Cedar Point Rockne and Dorais worked and reworked their passing combination to precision.

Far left: *Notre Dame team captain and quarterback, Gus Dorais led the 35-13 win over Army in 1913 that brought the Irish national recognition.*

Below: *On their way to smashing Marquette 69-0 at White Sox Park in Chicago on Thanksgiving Day, 1912, end Knute Rockne clears the way for fullback Ray Eichenlaub.*

Right: *As an alumnus, Gus Dorais demonstrates his forward pass at a football clinic being conducted by coach and former teammate Knute Rockne.*

Far right: *Notre Dame's football coach from 1913 through 1917, Jesse Harper helped establish the winning Irish tradition, compiling a 34-5-1 record during his tenure there. Harper helped Knute Rockne land the assistant coach position in 1914.*

Their effort is also credited with producing the buttonhook play, where the receiver curls back to take the pass while using his body to shield the ball from the defender.

On the field, Harper's team tested its power against Midwest opponents while continuing to develop its secret weapon for the 1 November game against Army. The Irish opened with an 87-0 butchering of Ohio Northern, then followed by downing South Dakota 20-7. When Army coaches scouted the third game, against Alma on 25 October, they saw Notre Dame's power ground attack – built around 6-foot-3, 225-pound fullback Ray Eichenlaub – romp, 62-0. The Cadets were expecting more of the same the next week at West Point. The

Army team enjoyed a position as one of the darlings of the New York press. And while Notre Dame was known to be a potent little team from the Midwest, neither Army officials nor the eastern football writers figured the visitors would provide much of a challenge.

The Irish fumbled on the opening series, and Army took over inside the Notre Dame 30. The Irish defense allowed only a yard and regained the ball. There, the Cadets immediately packed their defense in tight to stop Notre Dame's powerful linebacks. So Dorais crossed them up with an 11-yard pass to Rockne. Mixing passes with runs from Ray Eichenlaub, the Irish moved the ball across midfield. On the next play

Rockne faked an injury, showing Army's defensive back a limp, then suddenly broke open in the secondary to take in a pass from Dorais for a 40-yard touchdown.

Army then scored twice but missed an extra point and led 13-7. Notre Dame answered with a drive and a score by halfback Joe Pliska to lead 14-13, an edge they held at the half. During the break the Irish rested on their bench with blankets over their shoulders, while Army coach Charles Daly adjusted his defense to a five-man front line. The Cadets, with one of their stars, Dwight Eisenhower, injured and watching from the bench, had reason to worry.

They opened with a strong drive to the Notre Dame goal, but Dorais intercepted a pass to prevent a score. Then he turned on an air show such as football had never seen. He completed 13 second-half passes. (For the day he completed 14 of 17, for 243 yards, amazing totals for 1913.) The effect of Dorais's success was that he opened up the power of the ground game, and the Irish double-punched the Cadets the rest of the way, winning, 35-13.

"Notre Dame Open Play Amazes Army," the *New York Times* declared the next day. Suddenly the little team from the Midwest was no longer an unknown. In fact, Dorais, Rockne and company had sown the seed of Notre Dame's nationwide following.

The Irish marched with that ebullient step over their final three opponents, Penn State, Christian Brothers of St Louis and Texas, to finish 7-0, the second consecutive untied, unbeaten season. Gus Dorais was named to the first team of Frank Menke's All-America squad and received the same honor from the International News Service (later to be a part of United Press International). Walter Camp selected Eichenlaub for his second team and Rockne for the third.

That spring Rockne graduated with

Left: Captain Knute Rockne leads Notre Dame onto the field for the first game of the 1913 season, against Ohio Northern. The Irish trampled their opponents, 87-0.

honors in biology, bacteriology and chemistry, and entertained thoughts of going to medical school. But by the fall of 1914 he was back at Notre Dame as a chemistry instructor, with duties as assistant football coach and head track coach.

Depleted by the graduation of Rockne and Dorais, Jess Harper's Notre Dame machine sputtered a bit in 1914 and finished 6-2. But the 1915 season held nothing but promise, although it dimmed a bit in the third game, when Notre Dame traveled to Nebraska and lost a close one 20-19. Still, Harper's third club gained another victory over Army 7-0, then bombed Creighton, Texas and Rice to finish 7-1. They came close to perfection again in 1916 but they lost their game with Army 30-10, to finish 8-1. Still, that finish was enough to bring Notre Dame another round of national recognition. Halfback Stan Cofall was selected to the Menke and INS All-America first teams. And Walter Camp singled out guard Charlie Bachman for his second-team All-America unit. Cofall set a record for points per game during his career, 246 in 24 games, for a 10.3 average. It has stood for seven decades.

Notre Dame's 1916 freshman team included an eccentric older player, George Gipp. He had come to school with a reputation as a fine baseball player and might have remained a baseballer if assistant coach Knute Rockne hadn't caught sight of him drop kicking a football one September afternoon.

Gipp moved to the varsity for the 1917 season, Harper's last, but he wasn't *the* star. That status belonged to center Frank Rydzewski, who would make the Newspaper Enterprise Association and INS All-America first teams. The Irish ran to a 6-1-1 record after an early tie with Wisconsin and a 7-0 loss to Nebraska. The high point of the season was a 7-2 upset of Army and its great Elmer Oliphant.

At age 33, Harper decided he'd had enough football after the 1917 season and went home to Sitka, Kansas, to manage his 20,000-acre ranch. In five years at Notre Dame he had compiled a 34-5-1 record, setting the school's dynasty in motion. He was elected to the National Football Foundation Hall of Fame in 1971.

As for Knute Rockne, he had just begin to earn his honors.

4. Rockne and Gipp 1918-20

Before leaving, Jesse Harper argued to Father John Cavanaugh, Notre Dame president, that Knute Rockne should be the next coach. Finally, Cavanaugh agreed. The decision would pay its dividends in trophies. National championship selection fell to a variety of parties in that era, as news agencies, publications, statistics professors and foundations picked a winner at the close of each season. Six times during

Right: *George Gipp played halfback on Knute Rockne's first team as coach in 1918. Though attending ND on a baseball scholarship, Gipp was recruited into football by Rockne and was key to the team's perfect 1919 season. The Gipper's outstanding play in 1920 earned him Notre Dame's first consensus All-America selection, shortly before his tragic death.*

Left: *Knute Rockne's excellent rapport with his football players helped him achieve coaching success. Here he regales a few with his unique brand of humor.*

his coaching tenure – 1919, 1920, 1924, 1927, 1929, 1930 – Rockne's teams were somebody's choice as national champions.

Yet even Rockne wasn't an overnight sensation. The World War meant that the 1918 season would be abbreviated to six games. In retrospect, it probably allowed the young coach to gain his footing. In addition to Gipp, Rockne's first team featured a strong freshman fullback, Curly Lambeau, who would leave school after one season and return home to Wisconsin to become the founder of the Green Bay Packers. In the first game, against Case Tech, Gipp showed his triple threat versatility. He rushed for 88 yards and two touchdowns, passed for 101 yards, kicked two extra points and punted eight times for 304 yards, as the Irish won 26-6. In the third game, the Irish tied the Great Lakes Naval Station Training Team 7-7. That Great Lakes team featured future pro football Hall of Famers George Halas, Paddy Driscoll and Jimmy Conzelman and would go on

Below: *The victorious 1919 Notre Dame team came out of the season 9-0. Key to the team's success were players George Trafton, Hunk Anderson, Roger Kiley, Pete Bahan, George Gipp and, of course, Coach Knute Rockne.*

Victorious 19 Foot-Ball Squad 19 NOTRE DAME

Above: *A crowd of 10,000 attended Notre Dame's first Homecoming, against Purdue, in 1920. George Gipp's 85-yard run set the stage for Notre Dame's 28-0 victory.*

to win the Rose Bowl at the end of the season. The next week, Rockne's team was upset by Michigan State in the rain, and after adding another victory, it closed the season with a scoreless tie against Nebraska. The 3-1-2 record was the last Rockne would see of mediocrity for a decade.

The 1919 team was flush with talent, including a number of veterans returning from the war. George Trafton, who would go on to greatness in the pros, played center. Hunk Anderson was a guard. Roger Kiley, Bernie Kirk and Eddie Anderson rotated at ends. Quarterback Pete Bahan was captain.

Gipp opened the 1919 season by rushing for 271 yards in two games. Then, in the third game, he passed for 124 yards, as Notre Dame beat a strong Nebraska team 14-9 at Nebraska. His best effort came

toward the end of the game, when he used his skill to run out the clock and protect the lead for the tired Irish. After that came wins over Western Michigan and Indiana and a meeting with Army. Gipp rushed for 70 yards and a touchdown and threw for 115 yards against the Cadets, as Notre Dame earned its sixth victory 12-9. He intercepted two passes and threw a touchdown pass in a 13-0 win over Michigan State, and followed that by completing 11 of 15 passes for 217 yards and two touchdowns in a 33-13 pasting of Purdue. When the Irish closed out their schedule with a 14-6 win over Morningside, Rockne had his first perfect season, 9-0. Strangely, there were no national honors for Irish players afterward.

In Notre Dame's first two wins of 1920 Gipp rushed for 306 yards and three touchdowns. In the third win, 16-7 over Nebraska, he passed for 117 yards and gained another 70 running. Then, against Valparaiso, he passed for 102 and rushed for 120 and two touchdowns. He bettered that against Army, rushing for 150 on 20 carries and throwing for 123 and a touchdown in a 27-17 win. He also returned eight kickoffs for 157 yards and two punts for 50 yards and kicked three extra points. "It was a show of immortality," commented the *New York Journal-American.*

The next week against Purdue he rushed 10 times for 129 yards, including one 80-yard run to break the Boilermakers' spirits, and completed four of seven passes for another 128. Only an injury could stop him, and it did in the next game. Gipp hurt his shoulder early and watched from the bench, his shoulder taped to his body, as the Hoosiers held a 10-7 lead into the fourth quarter. With Notre Dame's unbeaten streak threatened and the crowd chanting his name, Gipp returned to the game as the Irish marched to the Indiana goal. He ran the five yards for the winning touchdown.

He was still unable to play the next week against Northwestern. Late in the game, with their team losing badly, the home crowd began chanting for a token appearance by Gipp. Finally, he and Rockne complied, and he promptly threw a 50-yard touchdown pass. Before the game was over

he would finish with 157 yards passing, as the Irish won 33-7 to finish their second perfect season under Rockne.

Gipp had contracted strep throat over the Northwestern weekend, and the illness persisted. Gipp begged off early from the team banquet two weeks later, and the next day he was hospitalized. He was too ill to enjoy his selection to Walter Camp's All-America first team, the first Notre Dame player so honored. Camp also distinguished him as the nation's outstanding player. For the season, Gipp had averaged 8.1 yards per carry, a record that still stands at Notre Dame.

With the infection and complications of pneumonia, his condition worsened. On 14 December, at age 25, George Gipp died. Rockne had a private visit with the athlete on his deathbed. Although there were no witnesses to their conversation, its content has become legendary. "I've got to go, Rock," Gipp was supposed to have told his coach. "It's all right. I'm not afraid. Some time, Rock, when the team is up against it, when things are wrong and the breaks are beating the boys, tell them to go in there with all they've got and win just one for the Gipper. I don't know where I'll be then, Rock. But I'll know about it, and I'll be happy."

Left: *George Gipp's parents at the cemetery after his burial in Laurium, Michigan. Gipp's premature death from complications of strep throat stunned the entire football world. George Gipp was elected to the National Football Hall of Fame in 1951.*

5. The Four Horsemen 1921-24

Despite the loss of Gipp, Rockne had plenty of veterans returning for 1921, including Roger Kiley and Eddie Anderson at ends, Buck Shaw and Hunk Anderson on the offensive line and Chet Wynne at fullback. Chet Grant had moved to the starting slot at quarterback, with Danny Coughlin and Johnny Mohardt taking over as the halfbacks.

They extended the winning streak to 20 games by blasting Kalamazoo and DePauw, then traveled to Iowa where the spell died at the hands of the Hawkeyes, 10-7. To their credit, they regrouped quickly, beating Purdue soundly and powering past Nebraska 7-0 at Homecoming in South Bend. They followed with an impressive string of wins, to ring up a 10-1 record.

Rockne's 1922 team would move on an infusion of sophomore talent, particularly four sophomores: Elmer Layden, who

Opposite top: *Irish fullback Paul Castner runs the ball during Notre Dame's 8 November 1921 defeat of Rutgers, 48-0, in New York's Polo Grounds.*

Opposite bottom: *Coach Rockne leads his squad in stretching exercises. The popular coach participated in practices, sometimes even setting himself as the target for tackles.*

Left: *Grantland Rice in action. The famous sportscaster coined the term "the Four Horsemen" in 1924 to describe the Irish backfield.*

started at left half; Jim Crowley, who backed him up; Don Miller, who started at right half; and Harry Stuhldreher, a backup quarterback. None of the four weighed more than 165 pounds or was taller than 5-foot-11. And only Layden, who was reportedly timed at 10-flat in the 100-yard dash, had any speed. Yet, Rockne would mold them into a finely timed unit, capable of brilliant displays of ballhandling.

The Irish bulled past their first six opponents, struggling only with George Tech, 13-3, then faced off Army in a scoreless tie. The next week, against Butler, Rockne lost Paul Castner, his triple-threat fullback, to a broken hip. The coach then shifted Layden to fullback, and the next week, against Carnegie Tech, the new backfield had its first playing time together. Notre Dame

won 19-0, and Rockne had a glimpse of his squad's future. But the picture dimmed a bit the next week, with a season-ending 14-6 loss to Nebraska. Still, the Notre Dame coach was reasonably pleased. He had finished 8-1-1.

As for Castner, his hip injury had brought an early close to a brilliant career. In the 1922 season he had returned 11 kickoffs for 490 yards and two touchdowns, an incredible average of 44.5 yards per return and a Notre Dame record that still stands.

Although college football coaches were becoming infatuated with the single wing formation, Rockne focused on developing the traditional T formation through a series of innovations. To make his young backs faster, he sought lighter equipment and less padding. (Not satisfied with his

Above: *Notre Dame's legendary backfield of 1924 – dubbed "the Four Horsemen" – pose for a publicity shot. Left to right: right halfback Don Miller, fullback Elmer Layden, left halfback Jim Crowley, and quarterback Harry Stuhldreher.*

speed, Stuhldreher did away with his padding altogether.) Rockne knew the secret of their success was timing, and heading into the 1923 season he drilled them repeatedly. From their T they would move into their Notre Dame shift, Stuhldreher moving just back of guard and tackle, Miller relocating at wingback, Crowley stepping in at tailback and Layden lining up behind the other tackle. In another innovation, Miller became the team's primary receiver, making him one of the first, if not *the* first, running back in all of football to take on the role of pass receiver.

In what was becoming characteristic Notre Dame fashion, the Irish ran past their first six opponents, scoring 195 points and allowing only 16. Then, for the second year in a row, they were upset by a larger Nebraska team. They finished off the year 9-1. Notre Dame had lost two games in two years, both to Nebraska. They were determined not to lose to the Cornhuskers again.

Nineteen twenty four was a glorious season for college football. Red Grange at Illinois thrilled crowds in the Big Ten.

Ernie Nevers worked a similar magic for Pop Warner's Stanford Indians. And by the third game of the season, the Four Horsemen, with the help of sportswriter Grantland Rice, would grab the nation's attention.

The Irish worked their ballhandling magic on Army on 18 October, winning 13-7. Grantland Rice dubbed the backfield the "Four Horsemen," and the Notre Dame publicity office posed them on horseback. From then on the season moved at a gallop. Soon the offensive line – Chuck Collins, Ed Hunsinger, Rip Miller, Joe Bach, John Weibel, Noble Kizer and Adam Walsh – was tagged the "Seven Mules."

The next week they beat a good Princeton team 12-0 before another Eastern crowd of 40,000, then subdued Georgia Tech and Wisconsin before another meeting with Nebraska. This time, the Cornhuskers came to South Bend, and the Irish took their revenge 34-6. By season's end they stood 9-0 and earned an invitation to meet Nevers and Stanford in the Rose Bowl on New Year's Day 1925, the only bowl in college football at the time. Warner, purveyor of the single-wing, unbalanced line, was eager to test his Indians against Rockne and Notre Dame.

Miller, who had been an INS first-team All-American for 1923, didn't repeat in 1924, but the other members of the backfield took up where he left off. Stuhldreher was a first-team consensus pick of *Liberty* magazine, INS, NEA, Walter Camp, the All-America Board and *Football World*. Crowley made four first teams and Camp's second. Layden made three first teams. Adam Walsh, the center of the Seven Mules and team captain, was named to the NEA and INS second teams and Camp's third.

With his flair for theatrics and surprise, Rockne started his second team in the Rose Bowl in Pasadena. Warner and Stanford responded to that by driving for a field goal and a 3-0 lead on their first possession. In the second quarter Notre Dame worked a 46-yard drive, and Layden scored on a 3-yard dive. When Crowley's kick failed, the Irish led 6-3. Minutes later, Layden intercepted a Nevers pass and returned it 78 yards for a 13-3 Notre Dame advantage.

Rockne's defense turned up another score in the third quarter, when Ed Hunsinger picked up a fumbled punt and ran 20 yards for the touchdown. Finally, Stanford drove and scored with a minute left in the third quarter, closing the gap to 20-10.

The Indians were driving again late in the fourth period, when Layden intercepted another Nevers pass and returned it 70 yards to extend the lead to 27-10, the final margin. "It was true we got the breaks," Rockne told reporters afterwards, "but we would have won anyway. It is one thing to get the breaks and another to take advantage of them."

Top left: *Team captain and center Adam Walsh led the offensive line of 1924, known as "the Seven Mules," to an undefeated season and national championship.*

Left: *John Weibel played guard in Notre Dame's outstanding 1924 line.*

Left: *Irish halfback Jim Crowley evades opponents in the 1925 Rose Bowl contest against "Pop" Warner's Stanford University team. Notre Dame won the hard-fought game, 27-10.*

6. Triumph and Tragedy 1925-30

The magic figures of Knute Rockne's 1924 squad were graduated, taking with them Notre Dame's depth and experience. Gone were the Four Horsemen. Gone were the Seven Mules. Gone were the top dozen substitutes. In came a set of new faces – Christie Flanagan at left half; Red Edwards at quarterback, backed up by little Art Parisien; Tom Hearden at right half; Rex Enright at fullback. And their 7-2-1 record wasn't bad for a rebuilt team. But Notre Dame's hopes were really pinned on the following season.

In 1926 they ripped Beloit (as Vince McNally returned two kickoffs for touchdowns), Minnesota and Penn State in quick succession, then ran aground briefly against Northwestern. But little Art Parisien came off the bench to throw a touchdown pass for a 6-0 win to keep the streak going. They belted Georgia Tech and Indiana before their rematch with Army in Yankee Stadium. There, a crowd of 65,000 watched Notre Dame avenge the 1925 humiliation 7-0. After a Homecoming victory over Drake in the snow, Rockne was feeling confident. His team was 8-0 and scheduled to play little-regarded Carnegie Tech in Pennsylvania the next weekend. Rather than make the trip with his team, he decided to scout the Army-Navy game in Chicago.

The Irish were shut out that afternoon 19-0, bringing a shock to Rockne and the sports world. He later apologized to his team for his lack of judgment. At 8-1, Notre Dame traveled the next week to Los Angeles to play Southern California. A late score by USC gave the Trojans a 12-7 lead, bringing Rockne to call once again on little Art Parisien, the 5-foot-7 reserve quarterback. He responded by passing the Irish

Right: *The stars of the 1926 Notre Dame team, Butch Niemiec (left) and Christie Flanagan pose before practice in preparation for their game against Army. Flanagan scored the only touchdown in the 7-0 Irish victory.*

downfield to the game-winning touchdown, 13-12.

Rockne used the summer of 1927 to catch up on his rest. That fall a veteran team returned, led by Christie Flanagan in the backfield and John Smith on the line. They had every right to expect a fine season, but in fact it was full of disappointments, and they finished 7-1-1.

The 1927 season was followed by Rockne's worst record. By the time they were set to face powerful Army in November the Irish were an uninspiring 4-2. Army was undefeated at 6-0, the powerhouse of the East that year, and again led by Red Cagle, who had destroyed Notre Dame the year before. Accounts vary as to when and how Rockne made his "Win One For The Gipper" speech. Some say he made it before the game, some say at halftime with the game scoreless. What seems certain is that Rockne related his deathbed talk with Gipp and told his players of the request: "Someday, Rock, when things on the field are going against us, tell the boys . . . ." Various witnesses said that players and coaches openly wept.

Another certain part of the record is that Notre Dame played an inspired second half that November afternoon, despite giving up a third period touchdown by Army's Cagle to fall behind 6-0. The Irish battled back with two scores to win 12-6. Running back Jack Chevigny scored first from one yard out and reportedly told his teammates, "That's one for the Gipper." The clinching score came when reserve Johnny O'Brien, inserted for one play, caught a 32-yard touchdown pass from halfback Butch Niemiec, bringing a round of celebration on the Irish sidelines (O'Brien would be known forever as "One-play O'Brien"). Cagle, however, returned the ensuing kickoff 55 yards, and Army immediately threatened. Moments later, when Cagle was removed from the game due to exhaustion (he had played the entire afternoon), Army could drive no deeper than the Notre Dame one, where time expired. "Gipp's Ghost Beats Army," The New York Daily News declared on its front page the next day. Perhaps never in the history of sport has an event soared so rapidly into the realm of legend.

But from that grand moment Irish fortunes again plummeted, and Notre Dame finished with a 5-4 record. The lone consolation of the season was the naming of tackle Fred Miller to the INS All-America first team.

Above: *After the 1926 upset loss to Carnegie Tech, Rockne's team faced Southern California for the last game of the season. Here, Notre Dame's Jim Morse starts on a touchdown run. The Irish won this dramatic game in the final seconds, 13-12, giving them a 9-1 season.*

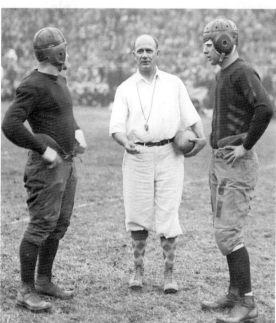

Above: *Notre Dame's Butch Niemiec readies to throw a pass against Army on 10 November 1928. Coach Rockne inspired his team to pull off the 12-6 victory to "win one for the Gipper."*

Right: *Notre Dame team captain John "Clipper" Smith wins the toss before the 1927 USC match-up, which the Irish won, 7-6, to end their season 7-1-1.*

Below right: *Notre Dame guard Jack Cannon was a consensus choice as first-team All-American in 1929. His performance helped the Irish become national champions.*

If Rockne seemed down for the 1928 season, things seemed even worse for the 1929 campaign, for college football's coaching celebrity was struck with painful, life-threatening phlebitis. But as Rockne had done in the past, he rallied, using the worst circumstances as the very material to motivate his men. The Irish also were helped by an immensely talented group of rising juniors, including Frank Carideo at quarterback, Moon Mullins at fullback, Marty Brill at right half, Tom Conley at right end. Another junior, tackle Frank Leahy, played as a substitute but would later emerge as one of Notre Dame's finest sons.

Jack Elder, a senior, had developed into a classy sprinter and needed all of his speed to dispatch Indiana 14-0 in the opener. He scored both touchdowns, setting a big-play tone for a big-play season. The poignant scene of the year came in an away game the next week against Navy in Baltimore. There, the players filed past a phone booth before the game, each to have a word with Rockne back home. With that inspiration, they toughened out a 14-7 win. After that Wisconsin, Carnegie Tech, Georgia Tech, Drake and Southern Cal fell to them in succession, and they headed into the season-ending Army game at Yankee Stadium with an 8-0 record.

Nearly 80,000 fought off the 8-degree weather to watch the two teams slip and slide on the frozen field. The signal event of the game was another big play by Jack Elder. As Army was driving to score in the second period, he intercepted a Red Cagle pass and returned it 90 yards for a touchdown. The 7-0 lead was all Notre Dame needed as the weather lined up with their defense.

A round of publications and foundations and systems awarded the Irish the national championship after the season. Carideo and guard Jack Cannon were consensus choices as first-team All-Americans. Tackle Ted Twomey was cited as second-team material by two other groups. On the season, Carideo had intercepted five passes and returned them 151 yards. He was also well on his way as Notre Dame's career punt-return leader.

The national championship was met by other good news heading into the 1930 season. Rockne had regained his health, and the stadium he had wanted so badly had been completed. Although Elder, the big-play man, had been graduated, Notre Dame's talented underclassmen returned as veterans.

In the first game in new Notre Dame Stadium Carideo started things off right against Southern Methodist, returning one punt 45 yards for a touchdown and passing for another, as the Irish won 20-14. They followed with a 26-2 demolition of Navy in which Joe Savoldi scored three touchdowns. While the home fire was still hot, they burned Carnegie Tech 21-6, then took their act on the road to beat Pitt 35-19. Returning home the next week, they blanked Indiana 27-0 and followed that by drilling Penn 60-20 at Franklin Field in Philadelphia. Next came easy wins over Drake and Northwestern, then another squeaker over Army in the rain and sleet of Soldier Field before a crowd of 110,000.

They closed out the season on the road at undefeated Southern Cal. Expecting a tough game, the Irish turned it into a 27-0 rout to claim their second national championship. Again Carideo was everybody's consensus as a first-team All-American. Left back Marchy Schwartz was also named to five first teams. A host of Notre Dame players – Marty Brill, guard Bert Metzger, end Tom Conley, tackle Al Culver, even Savoldi – received All-America second-team mention. Metzger was named to the AP and UPI first teams.

It had been a happy season for Rockne, perhaps the happiest of his life. On 31 March he boarded Transcontinental-Western Flight 599 from Kansas City to Los Angeles, heading for the West Coast to make an instructional film on football. Not long after becoming airborne the plane encountered a storm and crashed in a wheat field just outside Bazaar, Kansas. All on board were killed.

"We owe him more than he could know," humorist Will Rogers eulogized from Los Angeles. In his statement Father Hugh O'Donnell, university president, said: "Nothing has ever happened at Notre Dame that has so shocked the faculty and student body. Everybody was proud of him. Everybody admired him. More than that, we loved him. . . . He was a great personality, with attributes of genius. His loss in many ways is irreparable."

Left: *A view of the wreckage of the tragic plane crash on 31 March 1931, in which Knute Rockne was killed. So well-known and well-loved was the great coach that Rockne's family received messages of condolence from thousands, including President Hoover and the king of Norway.*

7. The Thirties 1931-40

The task of following Knute Rockne fell to his assistant, Heartly "Hunk" Anderson, the All-American guard who played for Rock from 1918-21. To give Anderson administrative support, Notre Dame officials brought back former coach Jesse Harper from his ranch in Kansas to serve as athletic director. But within three seasons the demanding Notre Dame alumni would call for Anderson's removal.

Considering the weight of the job, he would fill in admirably, but Notre Dame football, particularly the 1930s version, dealt not in what was admirable, only in what was great.

The 1931 team jelled around senior center and captain Tommy Yarr, a future All-American. The other veterans on the line included Ed Kosky, Al Culver and Joe Kurth. Marchy Schwartz, who had averaged an incredible 7.5 yards per carry while rushing for 927 yards in 1930, returned at left half.

Going into their 21 November home game with Southern Cal, they were 6-0-1 and favored. The Trojans attracted the first capacity crowd (50,731) in the short history of Notre Dame Stadium. It watched the Irish control for three quarters, mounting a 14-0 lead well into the third quarter. USC scored but muffed the conversion, to pull to 14-6 about halfway through the final period. They held Notre Dame on downs, regained the ball and drove for the score to pull within one at 14-13. Again Notre Dame couldn't get a first down, and the capacity crowd sat silent and stunned as the Trojans completed a long pass to set up the winning field goal as time expired. That loss was followed by a season-ending defeat at the hands of Army in Yankee Stadium. Coming out of the Rockne tragedy, Anderson's first team had finished 6-2-1, fine for most

Above: *The 1931 ND coaching staff, left to right: Jesse Harper, athletic director; Hunk Anderson, head coach; Jack Chevigny, assistant coach; and Tommy Yarr, captain and center.*

Right: *Notre Dame scores against Southern Cal on 21 November 1931. The Irish lost, 14-16, on their way to a 6-2-1 season, their first under Coach Anderson.*

American colleges but the kind of record that brought nothing but grumbles from the alumni.

In 1932 Kurth led a returning group of veterans that included fullback George Melinkovich, quarterback Chuck Jask and end Ed Kosky. They outscored their first three opponents – Haskell, Drake and Carnegie Tech – 177-0 before being upset by coach Jock Sutherland's Pitt Panthers in a road game 12-0. The Irish rebounded with wins over Kansas, Northwestern, Navy and Army before losing yet another season-ending game to Southern Cal 13-0, to finish 7-2.

While Anderson hadn't won championships in his first two seasons, he had at least established a sense of status quo. Yet all of that fell apart with remarkable rapidity in 1933. The Irish opened the season with a scoreless tie with Kansas, then righted their floundering ship by whipping Indiana, only to stumble into the worst losing streak in school history, leaving them 2-5-1 going into their final game with Army at Yankee Stadium. Although it wasn't announced, the season had already cost Anderson his job.

The Irish appeared headed for a final insult when the Cadets took a 12-0 lead in the third quarter. Nothing was mentioned about the Gipper, but he probably smiled again somewhere as, toward the end of the period, the Notre Dame offense found its footing to begin a drive culminating in a scoring dive by senior fullback Nick Lukats early in the fourth period. With the score 12-7 the Irish defense toughened, and

several minutes later Notre Dame end Wayne Millner blocked a punt and recovered it in the end zone, and although the conversion failed, it was enough for a 13-12 victory.

Army coach Gar Davidson entered the Notre Dame locker room and congratulated Anderson. "That was as fine a Notre Dame team as I have ever seen play," he said. "I don't see why you people always save it up for us. But we are proud to lose to a team as good as yours."

A week later, Father John O'Hara, Notre Dame's interim president, announced what had been rumored: "The University of Notre Dame has accepted the resignation of Jesse Harper and Heartley Anderson as athletic director and head football coach and has signed Elmer Layden for a contract that governs both positions. The university also has approved the selection of Joseph Boland as assistant football coach."

Notre Dame had hitched its future to one of its surviving legends. But while Layden returned the Golden Dome to the habit of winning, he still failed to deliver that unbeaten, championship perfection that the alumni had grown accustomed to under Rockne. More than anything, Layden failed to produce the type of superlative offensive performer, or offensive-minded team, needed to lift the Irish to greatness. Nothing, perhaps, is more indicative of this than the fact that his most heralded player was Bill Shakespeare, who finished third in the 1935 voting for the Heisman Trophy. Shakespeare, a 5-foot-1, 180-pound left half, affectionately dubbed "the Bard" (he was

Above: In the 1932 Notre Dame-Carnegie Tech game, Steve Banas of the Fighting Irish carries the ball for a nine-yard gain in the first quarter. Notre Dame whipped their adversaries, 42-0, and came out of the season 7-2.

Right: *Delirious Notre Dame fans demolish the goalposts at Yankee Stadium after their team came from behind in the last quarter to defeat Army 13-12, in the exciting 1933 match-up.*

Below: *Former member of Notre Dame's famous Four Horsemen backfield, Elmer Layden took over the coaching reins in 1934. Layden lasted for seven seasons, compiling a 47-13-3 record for a .770 winning percentage.*

reported to have struggled with English classes), was known primarily for his punting. In fact, he holds the record for the two longest punts in Notre Dame history: 86 yards against Pitt in 1935 and 75 yards against Navy the same season.

Layden lost his first game 7-6 to Texas, coached by Hunk Anderson's former assistant, Jack Chevigny. By mid-season the Irish were 3-3. They trailed Northwestern 7-0 in the second half and appeared headed toward more disappointment, when they suddenly broke loose for a 20-7 win. With solid wins over Army and Southern Cal, they finished 6-3.

That spring brought more sad news with the death from pneumonia of captain-elect Joe Sullivan. With the players dedicating their efforts to him, the winning streak carried right on through into 1935, as they rolled past Kansas, Carnegie Tech, Wisconsin, Pitt and Navy. Sporting a 5-0 record they faced unbeaten Ohio State on 2 November. The favored Buckeyes pushed to a 13-0 lead by the end of the third quarter. In the fourth quarter the Irish rallied and brought the score to 13-12. With 30 seconds to go, Shakespeare threw the ball right to Ohio State's Dick Beltz, but the defender was so surprised he dropped the ball. Given a reprieve, Shakespeare found end Wayne Millner in the end zone for the winning TD on the next play. "I've thought a lot about the pass," Shakespeare said later. "But I wake up nights dreaming about the one before it – the one the Ohio State guy had in his hands and dropped."

The Irish were unexpectedly 6-0 and seemed headed toward a banner season. Then came an unexpected home loss to Northwestern, followed by a 6-6 tie with Army in Yankee Stadium. They finished 7-1-1 after a season-ending win over Southern Cal in Notre Dame Stadium.

The 1936 and 1937 seasons were bittersweet for Layden as both teams finished 6-2-1, both with losses to Jock Sutherland's Pitt powerhouses. The highlight of 1936 was a 26-6 upset of top-ranked Northwestern in Notre Dame Stadium.

The 1938 team was obviously Layden's best, using a sound defense to rip off eight straight wins. By the seventh week of the season the Irish had moved to the top spot in the polls. For Notre Dame's 300th all-time victory, they hammered 12th-ranked Minnesota 19-0. Next they slipped past 16th-ranked Northwestern 9-7 and needed to beat eighth-ranked USC in the final game to claim the national championship. The Trojans, however, dominated 13-0, to dash the Irish hopes completely.

Layden finished his tenure with another pair of book-end seasons in 1939 and 1940. Both teams finished 7-2. Layden had worked under long-term contracts at Notre Dame, but when school officials offered him only a one-year deal at the end of the 1940 season he decided to accept the post of commissioner of the National Football League. Once again, school officials began combing the ranks of its former players who had gone on to coaching success. As always, Notre Dame was looking for its next legend.

Left: *Notre Dame's kicking ace Bill Shakespeare demonstrates his punting style in 1935, the year he finished third in voting for the Heisman Trophy. The Bard's 86- and 81-yard punts that season set Notre Dame records that still stand.*

Below: *Notre Dame makes a gain through the line during the 1938 game against Carnegie Tech, which the Irish won, 7-0.*

8. The Coming of Frank Leahy 1941-45

Below: *Members of the 1941 ND football team – left to right: Steve Juzwik, Robert Hargraves, Angelo Bertelli, and John Warner – hurdle over the season's opponents.*

Opposite top: *QB Angelo Bertelli on the sidelines during the 1943 Navy game in which he threw three TD passes and scored the final TD himself.*

Opposite bottom: *ND guard Pat Filley (52) opens up a hole for fullback Jim Mello during the 1943 50-0 rout of Wisconsin.*

Notre Dame officials were of course expecting another Knute Rockne when they hired Frank Leahy to run their football program in 1941. From the perspective of history, it seems they got that and more. Rockne's winning percentage was slightly better. But in 11 seasons Leahy gave the Golden Dome six undefeated seasons, five national championships, four Heisman Trophy winners and another grand chapter in the Irish book of legends.

Despite the dislocations of world war, Leahy accomplished all that with a personal drive that burned so hot it almost consumed him. "I used to think I was the most intense coach in the business," Army's Red Blaik once said of Leahy. "But I'm about ready to concede that Frank eats his heart out even more than I do."

After his graduation from Notre Dame, Leahy had served as a line coach at Georgetown, Michigan and Fordham. In 1938 he had become head coach at Boston College,

and in two years there he had run up a 20-2 record. Although he had just signed a new long-term contract with Boston College, Leahy had gained his release and accepted when Notre Dame came courting.

His first priority was to rebuild the Irish offensive, which he accomplished without changing Notre Dame's single-wing, shifting formation. The secret was a sophomore tailback, a 6-foot-1, 173-pound Italian kid from Springfield, Massachusetts, Angelo Bertelli. Throwing from the tailback slot, Bertelli became Notre Dame's first 1000-yard passer, completing 70 of 123 attempts (.569 percentage) for 1027 yards and eight touchdowns, enough to lead the Fighting Irish to an unexpected 8-0-1 season.

Leahy's great move came in his planning for the next season. The game of college football was changing, and he saw the need to discard Notre Dame's traditional offense. Bertelli was a fine passer but a mediocre runner, and Leahy felt the new T-formation

with split wings would serve his talents better. Bertelli could function as a drop-back passer after taking the ball under center. Soon sportswriters were marveling at this new concept, a "pocket" formed by blockers from which Bertelli could pass. There was some grumbling among Notre Dame supporters, and it grew louder when the Irish tied Wisconsin in the first game and were upset by George Tech in the second. The third game, however, made converts as Bertelli threw a school-record four touchdown passes and kicked three extra points in a 27-0 defeat of the Stanford Indians, coached by Marchy Schwartz.

The Irish finished 7-2-2, and Bertelli had thrown for another 1044 yards and 11 touchdowns. He finished sixth in the Heisman voting and received mention on several All-America teams. Bertelli also intercepted eight passes over the season, a school record. End Bob Dove was again a consen-

Above: *Quarterback Frank Dancewicz of Notre Dame kicks out of danger in the second quarter of the 1945 Army game at Yankee Stadium. The powerful Army team humiliated Notre Dame, 48-0.*

Right: *Coach Frank Leahy and quarterback John Lujack talk in the locker room. Lujack, who replaced Bertelli during the 1943 season, also went into the service the following year – but not before impressing the football world with his brilliant play.*

Left: *Notre Dame's head coach for 1945, Hugh Devore (left) poses with assistant coaches Gene Ronzani (center) and Wally Zeimba on the first day of the team's spring training session. Devore's team finished the season 7-2-1.*

sus choice, making the first unit of six different teams.

The next year might have been all Bertelli had there not been a war going on. Across the country, players were leaving the ranks of their college teams for military service. Bertelli lasted the first six games of 1943 before being drafted into the Marine Corps, enough time to burn Notre Dame's first six opponents for 511 yards passing and 10 touchdowns.

Bertelli was then replaced by sophomore John Lujack, a Pennsylvania schoolboy wonder. In his first game against third-ranked Army, Lujack ran for one touchdown, passed for two more and intercepted a pass, as Notre Dame won 26-0. With that confidence, Lujack directed the Irish to wins over eighth-ranked Northwestern and the second-ranked Iowa Pre-Flight School, 14-13. But a late score by the Great Lakes team ended Notre Dame's hopes of a perfect season with a 19-14 loss. Regardless, the Irish at 9-1 were the unanimous choice as national champions.

Despite missing the last four games, Bertelli was the runaway winner of the Heisman, polling 648 votes. Teammate Creighton Miller, who had rushed for 911 yards and 13 touchdowns and had intercepted six passes, finished fourth, with 134 votes.

Although Bertelli was named to the second-team Associated Press All-America squad, he finished first on most other lists. Miller, end John Yonakor (who caught 15 passes for 323 yards and four touchdowns), tackle Jim White and guard Pat Filley were all named to All-America first teams.

As it did everywhere, World War II brought its turmoil to Notre Dame football in 1944 and 1945. Both Leahy and Lujack went into the service, along with a host of other Notre Dame players. Frank Dancewicz became quarterback for 1944 and threw for 989 yards. Ed McKeever, Leahy's assistant, served as coach for a season of highs and lows. By blistering their first five opponents, the 1944 Irish shoved their way to the top ranking in the polls, only to fall in a 32-13 upset to sixth-ranked Navy. The next week, the new number-one team, Army, and the great Doc Blanchard humiliated Notre Dame 59-0. The Irish regrouped for three final wins to finish 8-2, but the memory of the Army defeat would stew until the next season.

Hugh Devore, a co-captain of Notre Dame's 1933 team and onetime Irish freshman coach, served as head coach for 1945 and watched his squad work its way up in the polls to number two with a series of five impressive wins. The surge stopped when the Irish tied third-ranked Navy 6-6 in Cleveland. Then once again Blanchard and Army humiliated Notre Dame in Yankee Stadium 48-0. Devore's team finished 7-2-1.

The war had thrown Leahy's great program into disarray, but upon his return the Notre Dame coach would astound the football world with how quickly he could reassemble his powerhouse.

9. The End of the Leahy Era 1946-53

Lieutenant Frank Leahy returned from the Navy in November 1945 to find a program well stocked with talent. For the 1946 season Leahy resumed his duties, and Hugh Devore, the war-time coach, moved on to become head coach at St Bonaventure. In Leahy's 1946 lineup Johnny Lujack headed a backfield of young talent with freshman halfback Emil Sitko and sophomore Terry Brennan. Behind them was nothing but pure depth, including speedster Coy McGee, Bob Livingstone and Corwin Clatt. Fullback John Mello had spent his war years playing with the Great Lakes Naval Station team coached by Paul Brown and would turn his experience and power into a key element in the Notre Dame offense. The line was a thing of veteran precision, with tackle George Connor, guard John Mastrangelo, center George Strohmeyer, guard Bill Fischer, tackle Ziggy Czarobski and end Leon Hart all on their way to earning All-America honors.

Beginning the season unranked, they blistered Illinois, Pitt, Purdue, 17th-ranked Iowa and Navy to move to the number-two spot in the AP poll heading into their 9 November game with top-ranked Army at Yankee Stadium. The Notre Dame offense was hitting on all cylinders.

As for the Cadets, they were riding a 25-game winning streak and had a pair of high-powered Heisman winners in their backfield in Glenn Davis and Doc Blanchard. They had generated 107 points against the Irish over the past two seasons. The sports minds of the day expected an offensive clash between Army and Notre Dame, and even Leahy suggested the two teams would score liberally. Instead, the teams produced one of the finest defensive struggles in college football history.

Below: *All-American and Heisman Trophy winner Leon Hart played end on four undefeated Notre Dame teams from 1946 to 1949. Hart was elected to the National Football Hall of Fame in 1973.*

Below right: *Tackle Ziggy Czarobski played for Notre Dame in 1942-43 and 1946-47, gaining All-America honors in his last two seasons.*

To make sure his team was fired up, Leahy had posted the game scores from the two previous seasons in the locker room. During practice, his players chanted, "Fifty-nine and forty-eight, this is the year we retaliate."

But the energy of both squads stifled the power of their offenses that afternoon. Neither team mounted a successful scoring drive. At one point the great Blanchard broke into the open, apparently headed for a score, but Lujack raced across the field and wrapped him up with a precise tackle at the Irish 37. With that threat snuffed, the game ended in a scoreless draw.

Yet, the game would prove to be a hinge in Notre Dame's swing toward the national championship. The Irish resumed their pace afterward, nailing Northwestern, Tulane and 16th-ranked Southern Cal by big scores. On the other hand, Army barely struggled past Navy 21-18 in a late game, and that played a major factor in the minds of the pollsters. They unanimously voted Notre Dame the champions at the end of the season. The Cadets' Glenn Davis won the Heisman, with Lujack finishing third in the voting. On the season, Lujack had passed for 778 yards and six touchdowns.

The 1947 season was perhaps Notre Dame's finest ever, as Leahy extended his unbeaten streak to 18 games. The nine opponents on the schedule fell by thundering scores – Pitt 40-6, Purdue 22-7, Nebraska 31-0, Iowa 21-0 and Navy 27-0 – leaving the Irish 5-0 and top-ranked heading into the Army game. There Brennan returned the opening kickoff 97 yards for a touchdown, and the Irish finally quenched their thirst for revenge against the Cadets, 27-7. The big win was followed by a letdown and the season's only really close game, a 26-19 squeaker on the road against Northwestern. The Irish dropped to number two in the polls but regained their top spot two weeks later by whipping third-ranked Southern Cal 38-7 in a game highlighted by Bob Livingstone's 92-yard touchdown run.

The Irish claimed several national championships, including the prestigious Associated Press award, but undefeated Michigan also received the top nod from three ratings systems. Lujack also outpolled Michigan's Bob Chappius for the Heisman Trophy in a year when Doak Walker of SMU, Charley Conerly of Mississippi, Bobby Layne of Texas and Chuck Bednarik of Penn all finished in the top eight. In addition to being voted the AP's male athlete of the year, Lujack was selected a consensus All-American.

Although Lujack graduated to stardom with the Chicago Bears after the '47 season, the 1948 Irish followed up his act with an outburst of offense, gaining a school-record 3194 yards rushing. At the center of the show was Emil Sitko, who again led the team on the ground. Against Michigan

Below: ND freshman halfback Emil "Red" Sitko runs back a Navy pass he intercepted 20 yards in the first quarter of the 1946 match-up. The Fighting Irish won, 28-0. Two-time All-American, Sitko was elected to the NFF Hall of Fame in 1984.

State he carried 24 times for 186 yards and a touchdown, a 7.8 per carry average on the day. He bettered that against Navy with 172 yards and a touchdown in only 17 carries, a 10.1 per carry average. Frank Tripucka had moved into Lujack's quarterback slot, and while he could pass with the best of them, he offered little as a runner. Still, he threw for 660 yards and 11 touchdowns, despite missing some playing time due to injury. In any case, it all fit together well enough to bring Notre Dame a 9-0-1 finish for the season, giving the Irish 28 straight games without defeat.

Irish Bill Fischer, Emil Sitko, Leon Hart and guard Marty Wendell all received All-America mention after the season. Michigan, however, claimed the national championship, with Notre Dame finishing second on the AP poll.

The Notre Dame fortunes fell into the hands of junior quarterback Bob Williams in 1949. And he used the opportunity to carry Notre Dame to yet another undefeated season while rewriting the school passing records. For the season, he would complete 83 of 147 passing attempts with only seven interceptions, for 1374 yards and 16 touchdowns and a rating of 161.4, a school record that still stands. As a team, the 1949 Irish averaged a 6.02-yard gain on every offensive play, another modern record. Against Navy, they averaged a whopping 10.2 yards per play. They scored a modern-record 53 touchdowns over the season.

Emil Sitko rushed for 712 yards, leading the Irish in that category for the fourth straight year. He also scored nine touchdowns. But the real sensation of the season would be end Leon Hart, who caught 19 passes for 257 yards and five touchdowns,

in addition to holding down defensive chores. At season's end the 6-foot-4, 245-pounder from Turtle Creek, Pennsylvania would receive a unique award for a lineman, the Heisman Trophy. He gained this status in the dying days of one-platoon football (he and tackle Jim Martin were among the last of the two-way performers for Notre Dame), when an end could be appreciated for the "whole" game, blocking on offense and rushing on defense.

The perfect season, however, had anything but a perfect aftermath. In fact, Leahy later remarked to confidants that he wished the 1949 season had been his last. The orgy of winning proved to be the last straw among the anti-football forces on Notre Dame's faculty. To them, it seemed the school had gotten far more recognition for its sports programs than for its excellent scholarship. They used their influence to force the administration to drop the number of football scholarships to 18, from a high of 32. Perhaps the only thing that kept Leahy from resigning was a promise to 1950 team captain Jerry Groom that he would stay through the player's senior season.

To ease the burden on Leahy, Notre Dame promoted Moose Krause to the position of athletic director, thus freeing the coach from the business distractions of managing the athletic department. Still, 1950 was a season to be missed. Notre Dame opened as the nation's number one team but barely squeaked past 20th-ranked North Carolina 14-7 for the 39th consecutive unbeaten game (the longest, by far, in school history). That streak abruptly ended in the rain at Notre Dame Stadium against Purdue the next week when the Boilermakers gained an overdue revenge, 28-14. Disappointingly, the Irish went on to finish the year 4-4-1.

Leahy was left wrestling with a destructive self doubt. He had worked incredibly long hours, endured huge levels of stress to build the program. Those around him worried about his health. As for the ever-demanding fans, they offered nothing but grumbles.

Leahy turned his frustration into effort and returned a team re-stocked with talent to the playing field in 1951. John Petitbon and Billy Barrett ran at halfback, with a sophomore substitute named John Lattner waiting in the wings. Neil Worden was the fullback, and John Mazur started at quarterback, with an eager young Ralph Guglielmi pushing him.

For the season, Worden would lead the team in scoring, with eight touchdowns, but he got four of them in the second quarter of the first game, against Indiana, as the Irish unleashed their pent-up anger

Below: Coach Frank Leahy poses with his first string backfield on the first day of fall practice, 1949. Left to right are halfback Emil Sitko, quarterback Robert Williams, halfback William Gay, and halfback Lawrence Coutre. With their 10-0 record, the '49 Fighting Irish were the unanimous choice for the national championship.

Left: *Notre Dame captain Jerry Groom smashes into the 1950 practice season as Coach Leahy and teammates look on. Although they opened the season ranked number one, the Irish finished with a disappointing record of 4-4-1.*

Below: *Heisman Trophy winner in 1953, John Lattner scored 120 points and intercepted 13 passes in his three years as Notre Dame's regular halfback. His stellar play in 1953 helped his team to a national championship.*

and pelted the Hoosiers 48-6. They treated Detroit in the same fashion, but then were upset by SMU 27-20, in Notre Dame Stadium. After big wins over Pitt, Purdue and Navy, the Irish suffered the worst loss of Leahy's long and distinguished career, 35-0, to fifth-ranked Michigan State. They achieved the 400th victory in the school's history with a 12-7 win over North Carolina the next week, then scored late to tie Iowa in Notre Dame Stadium. Having struggled back to respectability, the Irish closed a 7-2-1 season with a 19-12 win over Southern Cal and Frank Gifford.

While 1952 would bring no immediate relief from the task of rebuilding, it was a benchmark year in another way. Reverend Theodore Hesburgh came to the presidency of Notre Dame, bringing with him Reverend Edmund Joyce as administrative vice president and chairman of the athletic board. Under Hesburgh, the university would prosper, and Notre Dame athletics would eventually find its modern athletic identity. It would be accurate to say that the two men helped guide the institution toward a balance that made the school a model for other universities. That, however, wasn't accomplished without occasional faltering in the athletic programs. On the field the proceedings were infected with a severe case of fumblitis.

Record fumblitis, to be exact, by both the Irish and their opponents. Over the season, Notre Dame fumbled a record 57 times, losing a record 29 of them. Their opponents fumbled 51 times, losing 28.

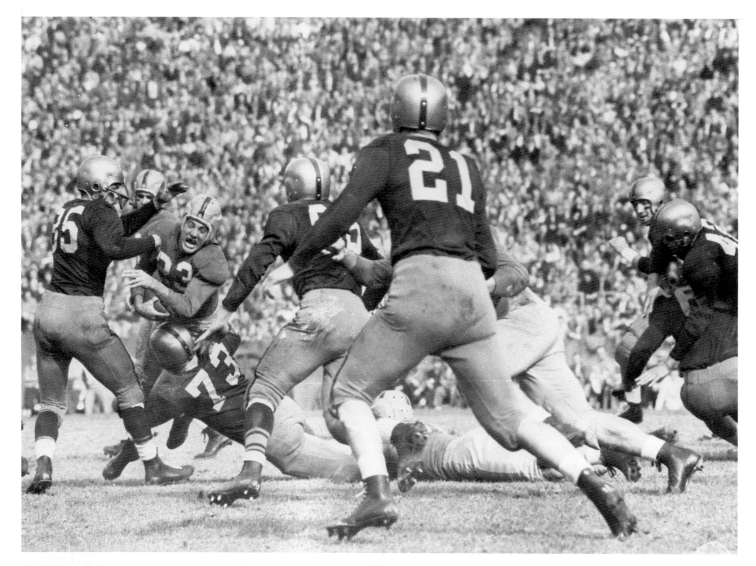

Top: *John Petitbon (23) is downed by Pittsburgh defenders on 20 October 1951. The Fighting Irish won, 33-0, on their way to a respectable 7-2-1 season.*

Above: *In 1952 Reverend Theodore Hesburgh – a champion of sports as well as academics – was named president of Notre Dame.*

Such statistics lead one to wonder how a team with that many turnovers could finish 7-2-1, yet they did. A large part of the answer was the emergence of a 6-foot-1, 190-pounder out of Fenwich High on Chicago's West Side, John Lattner. He mastered several trades for the Irish, running, catching and punting, enough to earn the Maxwell Award as college football's top player for 1952, his junior season.

With Lattner in the offensive backfield were quarterback Ralph Guglielmi, left half Joe Heap and fullback Neil Worden. Art Hunter returned to lead the offensive line, moving from center to end. On defense, the main man was linebacker Dan Shannon.

Leahy had braced for what he figured to be his worst season. First, the scholarship reduction had begun to take its toll just as the schedule became much tougher. When all was said and done, and Notre Dame had survived, Leahy ranked 1952 as his best coaching job. Considering he spent much of the year plagued by nervous exhaustion, it easily was.

The entire backfield and just about all the line returned in 1953. (Among the line substitutes was Wayne Edmonds, Notre Dame's first black varsity player.) The sports media acknowledged the Irish potential by ranking them number one heading into the season. Still, it was a strange year. The Irish opened the schedule with an immediate test, a road game with sixth-ranked Oklahoma. It was a seesaw afternoon, with Notre Dame scoring first and the Sooners playing catch-up. The score was last tied at 14. On the day, Guglielmi threw three touchdown passes to Heap, as Notre Dame won, 28-21. After that Pitt and Purdue were the victims. Then the Irish faced fourth-ranked Georgia Tech in Notre Dame Stadium. The Wreck was sporting a 31-game unbeaten streak, but Lattner returned the opening kickoff 80 yards to get the Irish going. On the sidelines during the first quarter, Leahy was stricken with severe chest pains and retreated to the locker room. There his condition worsened to the point that Father Joyce administered last rites. Word of his condition broke among the players, charging them to a 27-14 win.

Leahy was hospitalized but was back out the following week. Friends and administrators tried to convince him that it wouldn't be so bad if Notre Dame lost a game or two. For him, there was little worse, and the team seemed to agree. From there, they ripped Navy, Penn and North Carolina, then stalled amid controversy and flat play against 20th-ranked Iowa in Notre Dame Stadium. The Irish needed a last-second score to finish with a 14-14 tie, but it kept them in the running for the national championship.

The next week Heap ran 97 yards for a touchdown as Notre Dame demolished Southern Cal 48-14. Then Neil Worden closed out his career scoring three touchdowns in a 40-14 destruction of SMU. With that, the Irish finished 9-0-1 and claimed several national championships. Maryland, however, with a 10-1 record was voted tops by both AP and UPI.

The coaching clock, however, had run out for Leahy. Early in 1954, he issued this statement: "The doctors advised me after my experience between the halves of the Georgia Tech game to give up coaching." And Notre Dame followed with this release: "The University of Notre Dame regretfully announces the resignation of Mr Frank Leahy for reasons of health. Mr Leahy has rendered valiant service to the University since 1941 as head football coach, and for a while, also as director of athletics. . . . More important, he has distinguished himself as a fine Christian gentleman who represented Notre Dame's ideals to millions of Americans, young and old."

When they hired Frank Leahy, Notre Dame officials were seeking another Knute Rockne. This is how Leahy's record compares with Rockne's:

Rockne . . . Won 105, Lost 12, Tied 3, Winning Percentage .875.

Leahy . . . Won 87, Lost 11, Tied 5, Winning Percentage .813.

Top: *During the 1953 game against Oklahoma, Notre Dame's Joe Heap catches a touchdown pass. The Fighting Irish would pull ahead to down the Sooners, 28-21.*

Above: *Frank Leahy poses with a newspaper announcing his resignation in 1954.*

Left: *Irish fullback Neil Worden (48) sets off on a touchdown run against North Carolina on 26 October 1952.*

10. Troubled Times 1954-63

Notre Dame astonished the sports world in early 1954 by announcing the hiring of 25-year-old Terry Brennan, the Irish freshman coach, to replace Leahy. But despite the surprise of the public, Brennan had displayed just the type of character that Notre Dame wanted in its next coach. A three-year starter in Leahy's backfields of 1946-47-48, Brennan had been graduated in 1949 with a degree in philosophy. He received a law degree in Chicago while coaching football at Mount Carmel High School, where his teams won three straight city championships. He returned to Notre Dame in 1953 as the freshman coach, only to find himself with the top job a year later.

From Johnny Lattner and Neil Worden in the backfield to Art Hunter on the line, Notre Dame has lost six All-Americans from its 1953 team. Yet Leahy's rebuilding efforts left the team with a substantial mix of young talent and veterans. Ralph Guglielmi returned at quarterback, and with him in the backfield were Joe Heap, Don Schaefer and several others. Most important, the offensive and defensive lines

Below: Notre Dame's 1955 starting team poses with Coach Terry Brennan. The backs in the back row are (left to right): Paul Reynolds, Paul Hornung, Don Schaefer and Jimmy Morse. Young Coach Brennan's squad finished 8-2 that year.

were stocked with veterans, including ends Dan Shannon and Paul Matz, guard Pat Bisceglia and tackle Frank Varrichione. The gem among the newcomers was a sophomore from Louisville, Paul Hornung, whom Leahy had projected as a future great for Notre Dame.

On reputation alone the Irish began the 1954 season as the nation's second-ranked team and promptly blanked fourth-ranked Texas 21-0. Then they rode into the hailstorm of 19th-ranked Purdue and quarterback Len Dawson, who threw four touchdown passes as the Boilermakers romped, 27-14, in Notre Dame Stadium. Brennan's Irish righted what was wrong from there and ran through the rest of the schedule, dropping Pitt, Michigan State, Navy, Penn, North Carolina, Iowa, Southern Cal and SMU, in order to finish 9-1 as the nation's fourth-ranked team. With his performance on the season, Guglielmi was the consensus choice as All-American quarterback and finished fourth in the Heisman voting, won by Wisconsin's Alan Ameche.

Hornung had seen playing time as both

Left: *The Fighting Irish opened the 1954 season by shutting down Texas 21-0. Here Notre Dame's Ralph Guglielmi (3) intercepts a pass intended for Texas' Howard Moon (center). Guglielmi's fine performance on the season brought him consensus All-America honors.*

Below: *In one of the few shining moments in an otherwise dismal 2-8 season in 1956, Notre Dame's Paul Hornung won the coveted Heisman Trophy. Hornung set a record by returning 20 for 556 yards, for a 28-yard per carry average.*

quarterback and fullback on the 1954 varsity. For 1955, he moved into the starting slot at quarterback. Jim Morse returned at right half and Don Schaefer at fullback, while Pat Bisceglia was the veteran on the line. But despite some fine individual performances Brennan's second team came to an 8-2 finish and the ninth spot in the final AP poll.

Hornung was named to five All-America first teams, including UPI. Schaefer, the fullback, made three first-team squads. And guard Pat Bisceglia was voted to the AP's first team, the only Notre Dame player so honored.

Nineteen fifty-six was a disaster. Perhaps it was the large number of inexperienced players moving into the starting lineup; perhaps it was the resignation of long-time Notre Dame assistant Johnny Druze, who accepted the job as head coach at Marquette. But after beginning the season as the nation's third-ranked team, the Irish finished 2-8.

As might be expected, the 1956 team set a record for kickoff returns – 49 in the season, for 1174 yards. Paul Hornung himself set a Notre Dame record by returning 20 for 556 yards, a 28-yard per carry average. He was named to the AP All-America second team and the UPI first team. But the real surprise of the season came with the Heisman voting. He narrowly outpolled Johnny Majors of Tennessee to win the trophy. "I couldn't believe it when they told me I'd

Above: *In the last game of the 1957 season, Notre Dame's Allen Ecuyer (60) drives past an SMU blocker to upset Wayne Slankard (37) after he made a six-yard gain. Notre Dame's 54-21 victory closed out their season with a 7-3 record.*

won it," the incredulous quarterback told a reporter the next day between classes at Notre Dame. "I did not think I was even up for consideration."

Meanwhile, Notre Dame tried to regroup its battered football program, and in fact Brennan did return the team to winning ways in 1957. The season brought a renewal of the Army rivalry, and after opening with shutout wins over Purdue and Indiana, the 12th-ranked Irish met the 10th-ranked Cadets in Philadelphia. Army took a 12-0 lead and stretched it to 21-7 early in the fourth quarter. Brennan's team rushed back with two touchdowns, only to lag behind at 21-20 when Monty Stickles missed an extra point. The sophomore end redeemed himself in the final moments with a 39-yard field goal for an Irish win, 23-21. From there, the Irish went on to finish the year 7-3. Guard Al Ecuyer was named to UPI's All-America first team, and to the casual observer it might have seemed

that Brennan had turned the corner. But it was not to be.

Notre Dame faced a schedule with six teams ranked in the top 20 for 1958. They beat three of them and finished 6-4. For the season quarterback George Izo, despite missing some games with an injury, threw for 1067 yards and nine touchdowns by completing 68 of 118 attempts. The post-season All-America mentions went to Ecuyer and end Monty Stickles.

And the pink slip went to Brennan, who confirmed to reporters after the season that he had been fired. In his statement on the matter Father Hesburgh said, "It is with great reluctance that I accept this recommendation. In the five years that you have been head coach of the university, you have impressed all of us as the kind of young man that Notre Dame aspires to produce."

Joe Kuharich, a veteran college and professional coach, was hired to replace Brennan. In four years, he produced a dismal

Left: *In the final moments of the 1957 gridiron classic against Army, Notre Dame's Monty Stickles kicks the 39-yard field goal that wins it for the Irish, 23-21.*

Below: *Notre Dame's quarterback Daryle Lamonica outraces Southern California's halfback Loran Hunt into the end zone for a first-quarter touchdown during their 1961 match-up. Notre Dame blanked the Trojans, 30-0.*

17-23 record. His first team (1959) finished 5-5. His second, with Daryle Lamonica at quarterback and Nick Buoniconti on the line, won its opener, then lost eight straight, to finish 2-8. With Lamonica and Buoniconti returning for 1961, the Irish climbed to 5-5. Then Kuharich's 1962 team performed at the same level, giving him three 5-5 teams in four years. Believing that his firing was imminent, Kuharich resigned in March 1962 and was replaced by old Notre Dame hand Hugh Devore as interim coach for 1963.

The 1963 season was one of few highlights. The 23 November Iowa game was cancelled due to the death of President John Kennedy. The Irish might well have wished to cancel the others. Notre Dame finished 2-7, although one of the two wins was an upset of seventh-ranked Southern Cal. Again, Notre Dame officials found themselves with the unenviable task of looking for another Rockne.

11. Parseghian 1964-74

Notre Dame picked Ara Parseghian, the son of an Armenian immigrant, as its next coach, and he quickly won his way into Irish hearts by becoming an overnight sensation. Those who knew Parseghian weren't surprised at his success; he had a football background steeped in excellent coaching. After service in World War II, he had enrolled at Miami (Ohio) University, where he earned little All-America honors. Just short of graduation in 1947 the 24-year-old Parseghian took up the offer of Paul Brown and the Cleveland Browns to turn professional. He played one year before a hip injury ended his career, then returned to Miami as an assistant to another legend, Woody Hayes. When Hayes left for Ohio State in 1951, Parseghian assumed the head coaching duties at Miami, where in five years he won 39 games and lost just six, a good enough record to earn him the top job at Northwestern. Not only did he revive Northwestern's program, his teams won four straight games over Notre Dame, a factor that led to his hiring in South Bend.

Parseghian made sweeping changes that spring of 1964, discarding the old split-T offense and picking up variations of the slot-T and I formations used by the pros. Parseghian had his mind set on the passing game.

His first real task was to find a quarterback, and amid the scrapheap of talent on campus he discovered one, a forgotten senior, John Huarte, who had failed to letter in 1963 as a third-string junior. Huarte had attempted only 50 passes in two varsity seasons, but Parseghian found him to be just the athlete he needed to run the offense. He could move and throw, and the only ingredient missing seemed to be confidence.

Over the spring, the Notre Dame staff worked intensively to school Huarte in the offense, to refine his skills, and to assure him that he would be the starter that fall. His primary receiver for 1964 would be another Californian, Jack Snow, who would catch 60 passes in the season for 1114 yards. The others in the Notre Dame backfield were speedy sophomore Nick Eddy at

Right: *The Fighting Irish squad works out under Coach Ara Parseghian's watchful eye in preparation for the contest against Pittsburgh on 7 November 1964. Parseghian would work more magic to coach his team to their seventh consecutive win, 17-15, on their way to a 9-1 season.*

right half, Bill Wolski at left half and Joe Farrell at fullback. Linebacker Jim Carroll was the heart of the defense, along with defensive back Tony Carey, end Alan Page and tackle Kevin Hardy.

Huarte more than fulfilled expectations by throwing for 270 yards in the rain as the Irish opened the season by whipping Wisconsin 31-7 in a road game. Snow alone caught nine passes for 217 yards, setting a new school record. The defense did its part as well, holding the Badgers to a minus 51 yards rushing, a Notre Dame record.

From there, the confidence grew steadily as they defeated Purdue and Bob Griese, Air Force, UCLA, Stanford and Navy by big scores.

This was followed by a 17-15 squeaker over Pitt, aided by Huarte's 91-yard scoring pass to Eddy and a late stand by the defense. From there, they blew out Iowa and Michigan State to stand 9-0 heading into their final game on the road against Southern Cal and fleet back Mike Garrett. It proved to be a heartbreaker, which Southern Cal won in the final seconds 20-17.

The consolations were nice and numerous, but somehow they couldn't replace a lost national championship. The Irish finished third in the final polls behind Alabama and Arkansas. The big surprise came when Huarte edged Jerry Rhone of Tulsa in the Heisman voting, one of the greatest surprises in the history of the trophy. For the year, he ranked third nationally in total offense, with 2069 yards. He was named back of the year and player of the year by UPI. Snow was named to UPI's All-America first team and AP's second. Jim Carroll was a UPI second teamer, while Tony Carey and Kevin Hardy received mention on other teams. The Football Writers Association named Parseghian Coach of the Year.

Matching the 1964 showing would prove impossible the next year. Huarte had been graduated to the New York Jets and was replaced by Bill Zloch, who was limited as a passer but full of heart and grit as a competitor. Wolski and Eddy remained the fixtures in the backfield, with Larry Conjar moving in at fullback. Dick Arrington and Tom Regner would lead a veteran offensive line. But the defense received a blow when Kevin Hardy was injured early on and missed most of the season. Going two ways, Arrington replaced him in the defensive lineup. Alan Page returned at defensive end, and Carey again was the man in the secondary.

All in all, it wasn't a bad year. They opened by blowing out California to move to number one in the polls, then lost the

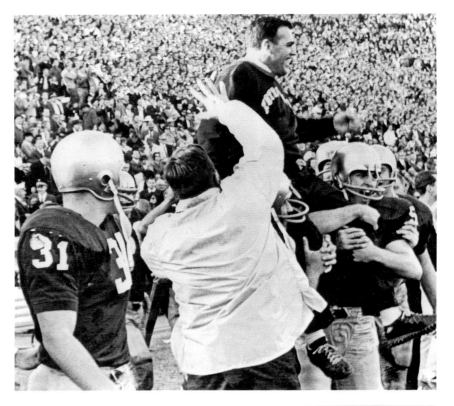

second game to Bob Griese and sixth-ranked Purdue 25-21. From there, they ripped through six victories, only to lose their ninth game 12-3 to top-ranked Michigan State. They closed out a 7-2-1 season with a scoreless tie with Miami (Florida) and a ninth-place finish in the polls.

The coaching challenge for 1966 was to find a passer, and find one in a hurry, for the Irish would open the season against Purdue and senior Bob Griese. Their top candidates, Terry Hanratty and Coley O'Brien, both sophomores, had no varsity experience. After evaluating both, the coaches went with Hanratty, a 6-foot-1, 190-pounder from Pennsylvania. He was matched with another sophomore, 6-foot-4, 210-pound Jim Seymour, to give the Irish a passing combination equal to Huarte-Snow. Nick Eddy returned to left half as a senior, and Rocky Bleier moved in at right half. Kevin Hardy and Alan Page returned to the defensive line, and Notre Dame featured an excellent pair of linebackers in Jim Lynch and John Pergine.

They exploded against eighth-ranked Purdue in Notre Dame Stadium. Hanratty completed 16 of the 24 passes for 304 yards and three touchdowns. Seymour caught 13 of those balls for a school-record 276 yards receiving and three touchdowns, as Notre Dame won 26-14.

They went on to win their next seven games by big scores, and excitement was high as they approached their 19 November meeting with Duffy Daugherty's Michigan State team, also undefeated, also rolling on the hopes of a national championship. It was, perhaps, the biggest college football

Top: *Elated Notre Dame players carry Coach Parseghian off the field after their eighth straight victory of the '64 season, a 34-7 tromping of Michigan State.*

Above: *Team captain and linebacker Jim Lynch earned a unanimous selection to the All-America first team in 1966, the year Notre Dame also received almost unanimous acclaim as national champions.*

game of the decade. The Spartans were led by their 6-foot-7 defensive end, Bubba Smith; the Irish by Seymour and Hanratty. Nick Eddy had an injured shoulder and was unable to play.

The second-ranked Spartans were primed for the showdown, particularly Bubba Smith. He knocked both Hanratty and starting center George Goeddeke out in the first quarter. Hanratty's shoulder injury finished him for the rest of the season. O'Brien, his replacement, had recently been diagnosed as having diabetes, placing a limitation on his stamina.

Michigan State ran out to a 10-point lead with a four-yard run by Regis Cavender and a 47-yard field goal by Dick Kenney. But O'Brien pushed the Irish downfield with a 54-yard drive capped by a 34-yard scoring pass to Bob Gladieux, Eddy's replacement. He again drove them into scoring position at the opening of the fourth quarter, but their progress died on the Spartan 10. From there, Joe Azzaro kicked a 28-yard field goal to tie the game at 10. With five minutes left, Tom Schoen intercepted a Michigan State pass and returned it to the Spartan 18. But State's defense threw back the Notre Dame offense, and Azzaro's field goal attempt from 42 yards was wide right. Late in the game the Irish got the ball back at their own 30 with time for several passing plays. But rather than risk an interception, Parseghian was conservative, a decision that brought rounds of criticism. The game ended tied.

The game settled little for college football, as the polls were mixed in their judgment. But the decision was made easier when O'Brien and the Irish hammered Southern Cal 51-0 to close the season at 9-0-1. They were almost unanimously acclaimed national champions. Nick Eddy, who had closed out a college career with 1615 yards rushing (a 5.5 average gain), finished third in the Heisman voting, and Hanratty sixth. The sophomore quarterback had thrown for 1247 yards and eight touchdowns, enough for mention on the AP's All-American third team. Seymour had 862 yards in receptions. Nick Eddy and linebacker Jim Lynch were unanimous selections to the All-America first teams. Guard Tom Regner was also a consensus All-American.

With two more varsity seasons ahead of them, the football world seemed to be Terry Hanratty's and Jim Seymour's oyster. They had been featured on the cover of *Time* magazine and publicized far and wide by the sports media. Yet they never quite realized their promise. The Irish opened the 1967 season as the nation's top-ranked team but lost to Purdue and Mike Phipps 28-21 in the second game. They finished the year 8-2 with a close victory over Miami, enough to earn them a fifth-place ranking in the final polls.

The same would happen in 1968, the senior season for Seymour and Hanratty. They opened third-ranked and full of steam, bashing fifth-ranked Oklahoma

45-21 in Notre Dame Stadium. But then Mike Phipps, Leroy Keyes and top-ranked Purdue ended their dreams again, 37-22. They pounded Iowa, Northwestern and Illinois in frustration, but then lost again to Michigan State 21-17. A victory over Navy gave them some hope, but Hanratty's college career was ended prematurely by injury the next week in practice.

He was replaced by a wiry little 6-foot sophomore, Joe Theismann, a nervy player who wanted fame so badly he would change the pronunciation of his last name from "Theesman" to rhyme with the trophy he coveted. The season ended, however, with the Irish finishing 7-2-1.

Hanratty's career closed with his naming to the UPI and AP All-America first teams. Tackle George Kunz and Seymour made the UPI first team and the AP second. In the

Above: *In first-quarter action during the Cotton Bowl on 1 January 1971, Notre Dame fullback John Cieszkowski breaks a tackle by Texas linebacker Scott Henderson and carries to the Texas five-yard line. Notre Dame upset the Longhorns, 24-11.*

tense, seesaw game that ended in frustration for the Irish when, the Longhorns leading 21-17 and 28 seconds left, Theismann threw a fatal interception.

Still, the junior quarterback had broken two Cotton Bowl records. He completed 17 of 27 passes for 231 yards, moving past the 228 set by Roger Staubach in 1964, and his total offense of 279 yards bettered the 267 set by Duke Carlisle, also in 1964.

Notre Dame's 1969 frustration burst into an offensive explosion in 1970, as Theismann set passing records, Gatewood set receiving records and the team set total offense marks. For the season, Theismann completed 155 of 268 passes for a school record 2429 yards and 16 touchdowns. Gatewood, meanwhile, caught 77 of those passes for 1123 yards and seven touchdowns. Theismann's season totals would bring him 5432 yards of total offense, then a Notre Dame record. Against Southern Cal alone Theismann completed 33 of 58 passes for 526 yards. In the second game of the season, against Purdue, Gatewood had 192 yards in receptions.

The great numbers, however, didn't always translate into big things on the scoreboard. The Irish zipped past opponents for seven big wins to move to the top spot in the polls. There, they struggled with Georgia Tech before winning 10-7, then grazed seventh-ranked LSU 3-0 to stand 9-0 heading into their final regular-season game with none other than Southern Cal. But as in the past, it rained on the Irish in California. The Trojans raced out to a good lead, then held on for a 38-28 upset. The Irish saw their national championship washed away in a California storm drain.

Their redemption came with an invitation to meet top-ranked Texas in the Cotton Bowl. Coach Darrel Royal's Longhorns came into the game with a 30-game winning streak and seeking another national championship. They left with the Irish brand still smoking on their rumps, as the Irish closed down all scoring in the second half and carried off a 24-11 upset.

Theismann finished second in the Heisman voting to Stanford's Jim Plunkett and was named to the AP All-America first team. He was voted second on the UPI team. Guard Larry DiNardo made both the AP and UPI first teams, while Clarence Ellis and Gatewood were UPI first teamers.

On paper, at the opening of practice, 1971 looked as if it could be a great year. Of 1970's 22 starters, 16 were returning, including receiver Tom Gatewood, defensive end Walt Patulski and defensive back Clarence Ellis. The big problem, however, was quarterback, where a group of newcomers were fighting to start. The result was a dis-

Heisman voting, Hanratty finished third behind O J Simpson.

With Seymour and Hanratty graduated, Theismann and 6-foot-2 sophomore Tom Gatewood became the Notre Dame passing combination for 1969. Around them, Parseghian rebuilt his team. Moving into the defensive picture were two super sophomores, end Walt Patulski and back Clarence Ellis. If nothing else, the '69 Irish got their problems out of the way early, losing to Purdue in the second game and tying third-ranked Southern Cal in the fifth. From there, they rushed to an 8-1-1 close and eighth place in the polls, as Theismann passed for 1531 yards and 13 touchdowns.

The season marked the first time in 45 years that Notre Dame had agreed to go to a bowl game since Knute Rockne took the Four Horsemen to the 1925 Rose Bowl and whipped Stanford. For the grand coming out the '69 Irish were matched against top-ranked Texas in the Cotton Bowl. It was a

appointing season, and the Irish ended 8-2 and ranked 13th in the final AP poll, the first time a Parseghian team at Notre Dame had finished out of the Top 10. Ellis and Patulski were both voted consensus All-Americans. And Gatewood finished his fine career with 157 receptions for 2283 yards and 19 touchdowns, an average of 112 yards per game.

For the 1972 season, Tom Clements, a fine sophomore, moved in at quarterback, with Cliff Brown as the backup. And Dave Casper, who would go on to fame as a tight end, played left offensive tackle. On defense, 6-foot-5, 265-pound Greg Marx, a co-captain, would earn consensus All-America honors.

The Irish won their first four before being upset by Missouri 30-26 in the rain at Notre Dame Stadium. They won their next four after that, but top-ranked Southern Cal and Anthony Davis overpowered them 45-23 in the last game of the season, for another 8-2 finish. But this time, when the Orange Bowl offered, Notre Dame accepted. Unfortunately, the Irish might have wished they hadn't. Johnny Rodgers ran wild in a Cornhusker romp, 40-6. Notre Dame finished the year 14th in the polls.

Art Best at left half and Eric Penick at right gave the Irish excellent speed. And fullback Wayne Bullock provided the power. Yet even with this balance of talent and experience, no one quite expected what the Irish accomplished in 1973. They closed out a perfect 10-0 regular season with a 44-0 thrashing of Miami.

On New Year's Eve, third-ranked Notre Dame would meet top-ranked Alabama in the Sugar Bowl. The Crimson Tide of Coach Bear Bryant was also undefeated. Quarterback Jeff Rutledge led Alabama's Wishbone offense, and oddsmakers considered it powerful enough to rate 'Bama a seven-point favorite.

The two teams gave New Orleans and the football world a classic to remember that night. Notre Dame struck first with a 64-yard drive fueled by Clements' passing. Bullock scored from the six, but the conversion kick failed because of a high snap from the center. Alabama took a 7-6 lead midway through the second period on a 52-yard drive. Notre Dame's special teams lashed right back, as Al Hunter returned the ensuing kickoff 93 yards for a touchdown. Clements threw for the two-point conversion and a 14-7 lead. Then, just before the half,

Above left: *Notre Dame quarterback Tom Clements spirited the Irish to an 11-0 season in 1973, a record that gained them almost unanimous selection as national champions.*

Above: *Notre Dame's speedy left back Art Best runs with the ball. Best was part of the first-class 1973 backfield, along with Eric Penick, Wayne Bullock and Tom Clements.*

Left: *Coach Ara Parseghian watches his team from the sidelines. Parseghian retired in 1974 with an .836 winning percentage and two national championships, after 11 years coaching Notre Dame.*

the Tide drove to a field goal and trailed 14-10. Alabama took the lead, 17-14, early in the third quarter with a 93-yard drive. Notre Dame got it back toward the close of the period by converting an Alabama fumble into a short drive for a score. Penick ran 12 yards for a 21-17 lead. But the Irish stumbled early in the fourth, when Bullock's fumble set up a short Alabama drive for a 23-21 lead. This time, however, the Alabama conversion went awry in the winds of the Sugar Bowl.

Clements then drove the Irish to the winning points. A key play in the effort was a 19-yard pass to Dave Casper, who had moved from tackle to tight end before the season. Bob Thomas booted a 19-yard field goal for a 24-23 lead. The climax came with Notre Dame facing a third and eight from its own two. Clements threw for the first down to sophomore tight end Robin Weber. With another first down moments later, they successfully ran out the clock.

The Associated Press voted the Irish National Champions. UPI however, voted the Tide tops. Mike Townsend was a consensus All-American for the Irish. Casper made UPI's first team.

Clements was back for 1974, as were Best and Bullock in the backfield. The Irish began the year second-ranked but couldn't maintain their sheen. They were upset by Purdue in the third game but held a 9-1 record going into their regular season game on the road with sixth-ranked USC.

With Clements throwing crisply, the Irish took a 24-6 halftime lead, but then came one of the stranger moments in the school's history. Anthony Davis ran the second-half kickoff back 100 yards, starting the Trojans on a 49-point scoring binge over the next 17 minutes. When quarterback Pat Haden and Anthony Davis were through, Notre Dame had been demolished, 55-24, one of the most incredible comebacks in college football history.

Two weeks later Parseghian announced his resignation, saying he wanted a sabbatical from football. Twenty four hours later, Notre Dame officials announced Dan Devine, a former head coach of the Green Bay Packers and the University of Missouri, would be the next coach.

The ninth-ranked Irish met second-ranked Alabama, led by quarterback Richard Todd, in the Orange Bowl. The Tide was a nine-point favorite, but after the Southern Cal debacle the Irish were determined to give their coach an upset victory to close his career. With drives in the first and second quarters, the Irish took a 13-3 lead at half, then held off the Tide in the second half to give Parseghian a 13-11 victory in his last game.

"This game ranks right up there among the greats in my career," Parseghian said afterwards. In 11 seasons, Parseghian had won 95 games, lost 17 and tied 4 for an .836 winning percentage, with two national championships.

Opposite:
Quarterback Tom Clements looks for an open receiver. Co-captain for the 1974 season, Clements' performance that year brought him All-America honors.

12.■The Devine Years 1975-80

Below: *As a veteran tight end under new Coach Dan Devine, Ken MacAfee turned in an All-America performance in 1975.*

Bottom: *Coach Devine leads the Fighting Irish onto the field for the 1977 season opener against Pittsburgh.*

A45-year-old father of seven, Dan Devine came to Notre Dame with a reputation for building college football programs from the basement up. In the early 1950s Devine had taken lowly Arizona State to the first undefeated season in its history, then moved to Missouri, where he coached the Tigers to the school's first football prominence. Compiling a 93-37-7 mark, his Missouri teams appeared in several bowls. But then Devine shifted in 1970 to the Green Bay Packers to take a turn at following the legend of Vince Lombardi. He experienced mixed results there (25-28-4 in four seasons), winning a divisional championship in 1972, but toward the end of his coaching tenure the rumbling of demanding Packer fans had grown even louder.

Devine knew that Notre Dame's fans would be every bit as demanding, if not more. Fortunately, Ara Parseghian had left the program well-stocked with material for 1975, including defensive end Ross Browner, halfback Al Hunter and defensive back Luther Bradley, all of whom had been suspended a season for university rules infractions. Other veterans from the Parseghian years included tight end Ken MacAfee (whose play would earn him a spot on UPI's All-America first team), tackle Ed Bauer, guard Al Wujciak and quarterback Rick Slager. The chief returnee was defensive tackle Steve Niehaus, a 6-foot-5, 265-pounder who would be named a unanimous consensus All-American for 1975 and finish 12th in the Heisman voting, a fine showing for a lineman. In the season, he would lead the team with 112 tackles.

The incoming recruits weren't bad either, including among them a solid fullback, Jerome Heavens. Then, of course, there was this matter of the young quarterback from Pennsylvania, Joe Montana, who had spent 1974 as a sub on the freshman team. Devine frowned at his practice

Left: *During first-quarter play of the 1975 Notre Dame-USC game, a powerful Irish defense swamps the Trojans. After leading 14-7 at the half, Notre Dame lost 17-24. With three players named All-Americans, Coach Devine's first Notre Dame team finished 8-3.*

Below: *Left half Vagas Ferguson runs over the Wolverine defense in 1978. Ferguson's brilliant career at Notre Dame extended from 1976 to 1979, ending with an All-America selection.*

habits, but there was plenty of athletic ability. And there was a void at quarterback. None of the veterans had emerged in spring ball. Finally, Slager was slated to start the first game.

They began the season ranked ninth, with a rare road game at Boston College and sputtered a bit before winning 17-3. The next week, Purdue was Devine's second win, 17-0, as Luther Bradley returned an interception 99 yards for a touchdown. Then Northwestern came to town and created Montana's moment. With the score tied at 7, Slager was injured. In came Joe, who whipped the ball around the field on the way to a 31-7 win. He did the same thing two weeks later in a game against North Carolina. Given just a minute of playing time late in the game, with his team trailing 14-6, Montana triggered an incredible 21-14 win, the clincher a pass to Ted Burgmeier, who ran 50 yards for the score (in all the play covered 80 yards). That game set the foundation of Montana's reputation as the comeback kid. Finally, with Slager as the team's leading passer (just under 700 yards) Notre Dame finished Devine's first season 8-3.

The next season had anything but a good start. Montana separated his shoulder in the opening game, as Tony Dorsett and Pittsburgh romped over the Irish 31-10. As dismal as the 1976 opening seemed, Notre Dame had the wherewithal to rebound. Ross Browner would have an incredible year leading the defense. And Rick Slager

Jerome Heavens at fullback (Al Hunter had been suspended for violating university regulations), the Irish rushed into the season ranked third. The only surprise came as quarterback Rusty Lisch, starter of one game in 1976, got the nod over Joe Montana at quarterback.

Things seemed stable enough, however, as the Irish promptly dumped the defending national champions, seventh-ranked Pitt, 19-9. But they were upset by lowly Mississippi the next week and seemed headed for the same fate against Purdue in the third game of the season. Devine tried three other quarterbacks before finally resorting to Comeback Joe Montana with Notre Dame trailing 21-14. In six minutes of play Montana threw for an amazing 154 yards, propelling the Irish to 17 points and an exciting 31-24 comeback.

From that point on, the job was Joe's. With Montana working the air game with tight end Ken MacAfee and split receiver Kris Haines, Notre Dame rolled to eight straight wins, including a 49-19 emasculation of fifth-ranked Southern Cal. For the season, Heavens rushed for 994 yards, and Montana threw for 1604 and 11 touchdowns. In a blowout of Navy, Jerome Heavens became the first back in Notre Dame history to rush for 200 yards in a game, reaching just that number with 34 carries.

In 11 games the Irish had racked up 382 points in offense, and the reward was a date with top-ranked Texas and Earl Campbell in the Cotton Bowl. Under the first-year coach Fred Akers, the Longhorns had won

Above: *Notre Dame quarterback Joe Montana calls his signals during the 4 November 1978 Navy game. The Fighting Irish dealt the Middies their first defeat of the season, 27-7.*

Right: *Game action during the 1977 Notre Dame-USC match-up. Devine's Irish, on their way to an 11-1 national championship season, crushed the Trojans, 49-19.*

got the job done at quarterback, throwing for 1281 yards and 11 touchdowns. Yet the real offensive wonders would be created on the ground, where halfback Al Hunter became the first 1000-yard rusher in Notre Dame history, with 1058 yards and 13 touchdowns. Boosting that backfield power was freshman Vagas Ferguson.

Again they finished the year 8-3, this time ranked 15th in the polls. The answer to their postseason prayers was an invitation to the Gator Bowl to meet Joe Paterno's young Penn State team, with Matt Suhey, Jimmy Cefalo and Chuck Fusina. Hunter keyed the Irish by rushing for 102 yards and two touchdowns, and Slager turned in a solid day, throwing 10 of 19 for 141 yards. Meanwhile, the defense intercepted two of Fusina's passes, and the Irish won 20-9.

The 1977 season offered plenty of good reason for high expectations. Devine had all 11 defensive starters returning from 1976's all-star cast, including Ross Browner, Willie Fry and noseguard Bob Golic. With Vagas Ferguson at left half and

Left: *Notre Dame and Michigan players clash on 23 September 1978, as the Irish are dealt their second defeat of the season, by a 14-28 margin.*

11 straight and were favored heavily over Notre Dame. But Devine used the odds-makers' snubbing in his pre-game talk, and the Irish brought the Texas joyride to a halt, driving the Longhorns down 38-10.

Devine said: "This game puts us where Texas was. We played the team that was rated Number One and beat them. Are we Number One? I leave that to the voters." The voters, it seemed, agreed, for they pro-pelled the fifth-ranked Irish to a unanimous national championship.

Likewise, Browner and MacAfee were unanimous All-America selections, with the tight end finishing third and Browner fifth in the Heisman voting. Bradley, guard Ernie Hughes, noseguard Bob Golic, Fry and Ted Burgmeier all received mention on one All-America team or another. MacAfee became the only lineman ever voted the

Walter Camp Award as the nation's most valuable football player, and Browner won the Lombardi Award as college football's best lineman, as well as the Maxwell Award as college football's outstanding player.

The sad part of the story, at least for Devine, was that just about all of them were graduated. Devine rebuilt his team for 1978. Golic, Heavens and Montana were the captains, but most of the other familiar names had disappeared.

They started off with losses to Missouri and Michigan, then rebounded to win their next eight games, only to be downed 27-25 in their final game with Southern Cal. The loss left Notre Dame 8-3 and headed to yet another Cotton Bowl, this time against ninth-ranked Houston.

It was a 17-degree day in Dallas, and the Cougars battered the Irish and their quarterback. Suffering from hypothermia and 96-degree body temperature, Montana was out much of the second quarter and all of the third, while doctors nursed him back to health with chicken soup. The Cougars held a 34-12 lead and the celebration had already begun on the sidelines when Montana returned to the game with about seven minutes left. The Irish defense quickly blocked a punt, which Steve Cichy picked up and ran into the end zone. A two-point

Right: *Notre Dame's Vagas Ferguson (32) brushes off the Trojan defense during their 1979 match-up. The Irish lost to fourth-ranked USC, 23-42, on their way to a 7-4 season, but Ferguson provided excitement for Notre Dame fans by setting a single-season rushing record with 1437 yards.*

conversion cut the Cougar lead to 34-20. After a short Houston possession, Montana whipped the offense right back into scoring position and did the damage himself with a bootleg from the two. That and his two-point conversion pass moments later narrowed the margin to 34-28. Suddenly the Cottom Bowl was on edge.

Houston coach Bill Yeoman gambled then, and with less than 40 seconds left went for a fourth and one at his own 29. The Notre Dame defense showed Yeoman nothing but snake eyes and stuffed the Cougar offense for no gain. With 28 seconds left, Montana and the offense had a chance to win it. Joe ran for 11 yards and a first down at the 18, then threw to Haines for 10. With eight seconds left, he missed on another pass to Haines, then another seconds later. Finally, with two seconds left, he completed the game-tying pass to Haines.

The score set up the extra point kick by Joe Unis. It was good, but Notre Dame was offsides, so the ball was moved back five yards and Unis knocked it up again, giving Notre Dame a 35-34 victory and Montana another chapter in his book of comebacks.

For the season, Ferguson rushed for 1192 yards and seven touchdowns. Montana finished off a 4121-yard passing career by throwing for 2010 yards and 10 touchdowns for '78. Bob Golic, with 152 tackles, was voted unanimously to the UPI and AP All-America first teams. Center Dave Huffman made the UPI first team and the AP second.

Unfortunately for Devine, 1979 was the kind of season to harrow the soul. Notre Dame finished the season 7-4 and out of the Top 20 altogether. It was bad enough to

drive Devine to announce his resignation heading into the 1980 season, effective at the end of the schedule.

In preparing his team for his final season Devine faced another choice at quarterback – between freshman Blair Kiel and senior Mike Courey. He resolved the question by using both, depending upon field position. With the graduation of Ferguson and Heavens, Devine had a new round of faces in the backfield. Substitute Jim Stone emerged to lead the team in rushing, with 908 yards. But kicker Harry Oliver was the big scorer, with 18 field goals. Linebacker Bob Crable again led the defense, with 154 tackles.

Considering the circumstances, it was a fine year. They beat Michigan and eight other teams but stumbled to a tie with lowly Georgia Tech and finally fell in an upset to Southern Cal in the last game of the season, 20-3.

The loss dropped them from second to seventh in the polls. Still, the Irish had a shot at the limelight. At 9-1-1, they were matched against top-ranked Georgia and Herschel Walker in the Sugar Bowl. They might have won the game if they hadn't given away two first-half touchdowns with turnovers deep in their own territory. The Irish outgained the Bulldogs in net yards, 328 to 127, but Georgia's 17 first-half points did the trick. Devine's final team went down 10-17.

A decidedly bittersweet chapter in Notre Dame's history closed with the final gun of the game. Once again school officials found themselves in the familiar guessing game: Where will we find our next legend?

Above: *Notre Dame's coach from 1975 to 1980, Dan Devine produced six winning seasons for a 51-5-1 record, with three Bowl victories and a national championship.*

Above left: *One of Notre Dame's brightest moments in the 1980 season was a come-from-behind, late-season victory over Michigan, 29-27.*

13. The Eighties 1981-90

Above: *Gerry Faust took over the helm as Notre Dame's head coach in 1981. Faust would resign after the 1985 season with a five-year record of 30-26-1.*

Right: *Coach Faust shouts instructions from the sidelines in 1981, his rookie season. The Fighting Irish opened with a 27-9 win over LSU, but hopes were dashed as they made their way through the losing 5-6 season.*

Opposite: *Notre Dame's tight end Tony Hunter was the key receiver from 1980 to 1982, when he won All-America honors.*

Gerry Faust, Jr, had rolled up a phenomenal record as coach of Moeller High School in Cincinnati. In 18 years he won 174 games, lost just 17 and tied two, for a Rockne-like winning percentage of .907, plus 12 city, five state and four national championships. Of his 174 victories, 90 were shutouts. Roughly 250 athletes who played for him earned college football scholarships to NCAA Division I schools. At the time of his hiring by Notre Dame, the only question about him seemed to be his lack of college coaching experience. In retrospect, it seems to have been a pretty good question.

He was a man of tremendous optimism and enthusiasm, with substantial gifts as a motivating speaker. He would need all these qualities and more. He inherited a solid array of good players, many of them starters for Dan Devine: Phil Carter at running back; sophomore Blair Kiel at quarterback; receiver Tony Hunter; kicker Harry Oliver; linebackers Mark Zavagnin, Joe Rudzinski and Bob Crable; strong safety Dave Duerson; cornerbacks Stacey Toran and John Krimm; and right offensive

tackle Phil Pozderac. With such talent, Faust had the framework of a fine team.

When they opened the season ranked fourth in the nation and played like it, whipping LSU 27-9, the uneasiness among Notre Dame fans settled substantially. There was still that hum of excitement the following week when the Irish moved to the top spot in the polls. Yet whatever Gerry Faust had going for him as Notre Dame's coach expired the next week, as 11th-ranked Michigan knocked the Irish from their perch 25-7. From there on it was largely downhill, and Notre Dame finished 5-6.

Faust warmed the fans again the next season, 1982, by starting off with four impressive victories, over 10th-ranked Michigan, Purdue, Michigan State and seventh-ranked Miami. Carter, Kiel and Hunter were all back at the skill positions, and with the wins hopes soared a bit as they moved to ninth in the polls. But again they faltered, finishing 6-4-1. It would be Faust's best record. If Irish supporters singed Dan Devine over 7-4, their irritation with Faust is easy to imagine.

Freshman Steve Beuerlein replaced senior Kiel at quarterback for 1983, and Notre Dame rode through another roller-coaster season to finish 6-5. Bud Dudley, the executive director of the Liberty Bowl and a Notre Dame alumnus, realized a life-long dream when he was able to attract the Irish to his bowl. It was an interesting little match, with Faust's team pitted against Boston College and Doug Flutie. Yet in a sense, the invitation to a lesser bowl only increased the irritation in South Bend. Nor did it subside when the Irish managed to squeak out only 19-18 victory.

For 1984, Faust's fourth Irish team offered a repeat performance, another 6-5 record and another invitation to a secondary bowl, this time the Aloha Bowl against Southern Methodist. The Mustangs ran out to an early 14-0 lead, but Notre Dame

Top: *Notre Dame president Reverend Theodore Hesburgh helped shaped the university's excellent sports program.*

Above: *Shortly after taking over as coach in 1986, Lou Holtz gives out sideline instructions. Holtz met the challenge of rebuilding the football team.*

Right: *Quarterback Blair Kiel calls the signals. During the first two years of Gerry Faust's tenure as coach, Kiel quarterbacked full-time. In 1983 Steve Beuerlein took over the position.*

battled back to tie the game at 17 in the third quarter. SMU pushed back to a 27-17 lead, only to watch the Irish pull up to 27-20, the final score.

Faust returned to South Bend to face incredible pressure heading into 1985. Still, he had a large number of lettermen returning, including senior Allen Pinkett, who would turn in a second All-American performance. Pinkett's career 320 points

scored would place him on the top of Notre Dame's all-time list. So there was hope, but it was a hope destined to fade steadily throughout a lackluster season. Finally, with a 5-5 record heading into his last game against the University of Miami, his optimism burned out. He resigned in order to give the school a chance to hire a new coach in time for recruiting. The Hurricane then humiliated Faust and Notre Dame 58-7 on

Above: *Talented tailback Mark Green runs the ball during the exciting season-ending Notre Dame-USC contest in 1986. The Fighting Irish won, 38-37.*

national television. It wasn't a pretty picture. Lou Holtz, Notre Dame's new coach, watched the debacle on television and for the first time he realized just how far he had to go.

Charged with waking up the echoes, Lou Holtz used the tool that had served him well at William and Mary, NC State, Arkansas, Minnesota and just about everywhere else he had coached. He tickled them with his sense of humor. In his career Holtz had been accused on many things, but pomposity wasn't one of them. And if Notre Dame ever needed a sense of humor it was in 1986.

Holtz enjoyed the early honeymoon, but

his first battle was to downplay expectations. "Many people who identify with Notre Dame believe in miracles," he told reporters. "I believe in miracles. But I believe they are not created by coaches." Holtz hoped to achieve competitiveness by selecting the team's best athlete and building around his talents. That athlete was Tim Brown, a talented junior receiver from Dallas, Texas.

Fittingly, Holtz's first challenge, Michigan, was Notre Dame's rival in the all-time college standings. In this game the Irish gained the edge statistically and outplayed the Wolverines. But they couldn't convert their statistics and early Michigan mis-

Below: *Notre Dame's wide receiver Ray Dumas accelerates downfield during 1986 game action. In their first year under Coach·Lou Holtz, the Fighting Irish finished 5-6.*

takes into scores. As a result, Michigan led 24-20 going into the game's late moments. Senior quarterback Steve Beuerlein moved the Irish into scoring position at the Michigan eight. From there he hit tight end Joel Williams with what appeared to be a touchdown pass. But the officials ruled that Williams' foot had grazed the out-of-bounds line.

Without the touchdown, John Carney kicked a field goal to bring Notre Dame to 24-23. But though they got the ball again in the dying seconds, the Irish couldn't kick another one, and the finished one point behind.

After that they would struggle to a 5-6 record for the 1986 season. The year would establish Tim Brown's credentials as a legitimate superstar, and Beuerlein would set career records in passing (473 completions for 6527 yards) and total offense (6459 yards). But for Notre Dame, a 5-6 record is far from palatable.

Heading into 1987, Holtz felt the weight of tradition upon him. "Our fans expect a minor miracle every Saturday and a major one every now and then." And if he didn't quite bring the ship in for 1987, at least he brought it within sight of shore. They finished 8-3 and received an invitation to the Cotton Bowl, reward enough in a year when team expectations were relatively modest. The real pressure was on Tim Brown, who was listed as the preseason favorite for the Heisman Trophy. He had broken Notre Dame's record for all-purpose yardage – returning kicks and receiving – as a junior. As a senior, he was determined to keep his focus, despite substantial media attention and high expectations. In fact he won the Heisman early in the season by returning two punts for touchdowns to kill Michigan State before a nationwide ESPN TV audience. But the Irish were thoroughly outclassed by Texas A&M in the Cotton Bowl. Even worse, the game was marred by an incident. The Aggies' 12th man, a player from the student body who is allowed to participate on kickoff teams, tackled Brown on a late-game kickoff, and seeing the opportunity to seize a souvenir, ripped the small towel from Brown's pants and attempted to leave the field with it. Enraged by the thievery, Brown chased him down and retrieved his towel. Hardly suitable behavior for a Heisman winner, many of the opinion-mongers tut-tutted the next day in newspaper columns.

Below: *Tim Brown poses with the Heisman Trophy he won in 1987. Notre Dame's sensational tailback also earned All-America honors for his stellar performance in 1986.*

Bottom: *Notre Dame's split end Pat Terrell makes the catch despite pressure from Purdue's Steve Jackson, in the 26 September 1987 match-up. Hopes rose as Notre Dame pulled off this third win of the season, 44-20.*

Above: *Notre Dame's Anthony Johnson finds a hole in the West Virginia line and heads downfield for a short gain during the first quarter of the Fiesta Bowl on 2 January 1989. The Fighting Irish topped a national championship season with a 34-21 win at Tempe.*

There were no lingering after-effects of that Cotton Bowl debacle in 1988 because Notre Dame won its first national championship since 1977 – and 17th in all – with a perfect season that was climaxed by a rousing 34-21 victory over West Virginia in the Fiesta Bowl in a game between the country's two top-rated teams.

Holtz placed his trust in quarterback Tony Rice, a fine athlete who was never fully accepted by Notre Dame's rabid fans because he was not a classic drop-back quarterback. But he was a whiz at running the option offense that Holtz so dearly loved, and he always seemed to come up with enough passing offense whenever it was needed.

The Irish started that season with a narrow 19-17 victory over Michigan in a nationally televised night game from Notre Dame Stadium. Reggie Ho kicked a 26-yard field goal with 73 seconds to play – his

fourth of the game – to provide the winning points after Michigan's Mike Gillette had pumped through a 49-yarder a short time earlier for a 17-16 lead. Still, the win was not secure until Gillette barely missed a last-second field goal.

The Irish defense was an equal partner in that team's success with its big plays during the season, including Mike Stonebreaker's 39-yard interception for a touchdown that secured a 20-3 victory over Michigan State, and Pat Terrell's 60-yarder against Miami that put Notre Dame ahead 21-7 in a game that was aptly billed "the battle for No. 1."

The bad feelings that existed between those two teams continued, with some pushing and shoving before the game, and then some rock 'em, sock 'em during it. After Terrell's interception, Miami roared back to tie the score at halftime on a pair of touchdown passes by Steve Walsh. Pat

Ehlers' touchdown and Ho's field goal gave the Irish a 31-21 lead in the third quarter, but Miami answered with another field goal before Andre Brown scored on an 11-yard TD pass with 45 seconds to play. Miami attempted a two-point conversion but Terrell broke up Walsh's pass to preserve the 31-30 victory.

The Irish also unveiled the most exciting player of the Holtz era in freshman Raghib Ismail. He had caught a 54-yard TD pass against Purdue, and in a 54-11 victory over Rice he returned a pair of kickoffs for 87- and 83-yard touchdowns, then added a 67-yard TD pass in a 21-3 victory over Penn State. The Irish tore up Joe Paterno's defense that day with 313 rushing yards and allowed only 128.

The Irish defended their first place ranking against No. 2 Southern California in the final game of the season in a contest that was billed as a battle of the quarter-backs – Rice versus USC's Rodney Peete. But it was Rice's show all the way, beginning with a 65-yard touchdown run in a 27-10 victory. Southern Cal was its own worst enemy – it outgained Notre Dame 356-253 – by turning the ball over four times, one of those a Stan Smagala 64-yard interception return for a TD that gave Notre Dame a 21-7 halftime lead.

In the Fiesta Bowl, it not only was No. 1 versus No. 2 for the national championship, but also Rice matched against West Virginia's All-America quarterback Major Harris. It was strictly no contest on both fronts – the Irish whipped to a 16-3 halftime lead, and Rice's 29-yard TD pass to Ismail put the game out of reach early in the third quarter. Rice finished with 75 rushing yards and completed 7 of his 11 passes for 213 yards and a pair of touchdowns.

Notre Dame was a solid pick to make it two national championships in a row in

Above: *During the 18 November 1989 contest against Penn State, Irish fullback Anthony Johnson stretches for extra yardage as he is downed on the 16-yard line. This gain set up a first-quarter touchdown on Notre Dame's way to a 34-17 victory.*

Above: *Notre Dame's sophomore quarterback Rick Mirer tries to escape the grasp of Michigan's Chris Hutchison during their 15 September 1990 match-up. Notre Dame won the hard-fought game 28-24.*

Opposite: *Notre Dame's phenomenon Raghib Ismail goes high for a pass over Colorado defender Dave McCloughan during the exciting 1991 Orange Bowl. Despite Ismail's efforts – including a 95-yard punt return in the final moments that was nullified by a penalty – the Irish lost this one 9-10.*

1989, and came to within the last game of the regular season of fulfilling that prophecy. The Irish opened the season by beating Virginia 36-13 in the Kickoff Classic, and then went to Michigan Stadium where Ismail astounded more than 105,000 fans and a national TV audience by returning a pair of kickoffs 89 and 92 yards for touchdowns in a 24-19 victory. Against Air Force, he returned a punt 56 yards for a TD, and added a 24-yard run for another score as the Irish won 41-27.

It was rarely easy for Notre Dame in 1989. Anthony Johnson's fourth quarter TD shook pesky Michigan State in a 21-13 win and his 14-yard scoring run broke a 14-14 tie against Stanford en route to a 27-17 victory. Southern Cal's highly touted freshman quarterback Todd Marinovich came to South Bend and peppered the Notre Dame secondary with 333 passing yards and three touchdowns – and was inside the 15-yard line near the end of the game before the Irish defense preserved a 28-24 victory. USC led 17-7 at the half but the Irish scored three straight touchdowns, the last on Rice's 15-yard run after passing 40 yards to Ismail.

After again tearing up Paterno's famed defense for 448 rushing yards, including 141 by Rice in a 34-17 victory over Penn State, the Irish went to Miami to challenge the Hurricanes again for No. 1. This time, it didn't work because Miami scored twice in

the fourth quarter en route to a 24-10 victory. The loss ended Notre Dame's 22-game winning streak, the longest in the school's history. The Irish then could only play the spoiler's role, and defeated unbeaten and top-ranked Colorado's 21-6 in the Orange Bowl, costing the Buffaloes a bid for a national title.

The Irish lost another battle to be national champions in 1990, which can aptly be dubbed "The Year of the Rocket," because Raghib (Rocket) Ismail was such a great offensive force for them throughout the season. Notre Dame had two bouncing-ball wins over Michigan and Michigan State to open the season. A deflected pass was turned into a 45-yard gain by tight end Luke Dawson to spark ND to a 28-24 victory over Michigan, with QB Rick Mirer passing 18 yards to Adrian Jarrell to set up the winning points. Another tipped ball set up the winning score a week later against the Spartans.

The game of the year was a 29-20 victory over second-ranked Miami. Ismail was brilliant, gaining 276 total yards, including a 13-for-108 rushing day and a 94-yard kickoff return that tied the score 10-10 in the first quarter. Craig Hentrich kicked a school record five field goals before the Irish nailed down the win on Rodney Culver's 21-yard TD pass.

The lead changed hands six times at Tennessee before the Irish won 34-29. Ismail's 45-yard TD run nailed down the win in the fourth quarter after his 38-yard punt return had set up Hentrich's tying field goal in the third quarter.

But Ismail's value really was proven as the chase for Number 1 came untracked in two games at South Bend where he saw little or no action. He was forced to miss a game against unheralded Stanford, and the Cardinals beat the Irish 36-31 in the final 36 seconds. Notre Dame had regained its Number 1 ranking by the 10th game of the season against Penn State, and The Rocket helped the Irish to a 21-7 halftime lead before he was forced to the sidelines again. The Nittany Lions then exploded for 17 points in the second half, the final three on Craig Fayak's tie-breaking, 34-yard field goal with eight seconds to play for a 24-21 Penn State win. With no hopes of being national champion, the Irish helped to decide the winner at the Orange Bowl when Colorado, who they had knocked out of contention the previous year, beat them 10-9 on the margin of a blocked extra point and Ismail's electrifying 95-yard punt return in the final moments that was nullified by a clipping penalty. With its moments of glory and pain, Notre Dame football continues to excite fans across the nation.

Notre Dame Fighting Irish Football Records

YEAR-BY-YEAR RESULTS

Year	Coach	W	L	T	Pts	Opp	Year	Coach	W	L	T	Pts	Opp
1887	None	0	1	0	0	8	1939	Elmer Layden	7	2	0	100	73
1888	None	1	2	0	30	36	1940	Elmer Layden	7	2	0	168	67
1889	None	1	0	0	9	0	1941	Frank Leahy	8	0	1	189	64
1890		No Team					1942	Frank Leahy	7	2	2	184	99
1891		No Team					1943	Frank Leahy	9	1	0	340	69
1892	None	1	0	1	66	10	1944	Ed McKeever	8	2	0	272	118
1893	None	4	1	0	92	24	1945	Hugh Devore	7	2	1	255	122
1894	J. L. Morison	3	1	1	80	31	1946	Frank Leahy	8	0	1	271	24
1895	H. G. Haden	3	1	0	70	20	1947	Frank Leahy	9	0	0	291	52
1896	Frank Hering	4	3	0	182	50	1948	Frank Leahy	9	0	1	320	93
1897	Frank Hering	4	1	1	165	40	1949	Frank Leahy	10	0	0	360	86
1898	Frank Hering	4	2	0	155	34	1950	Frank Leahy	4	4	1	139	140
1899	James McWeeney	6	3	1	169	55	1951	Frank Leahy	7	2	1	241	122
1900	Patrick O'Dea	6	3	1	261	73	1952	Frank Leahy	7	2	1	183	108
1901	Patrick O'Dea	8	1	1	145	19	1953	Frank Leahy	9	0	1	317	139
1902	James Faragher	6	2	1	203	51	1954	Terry Brennan	9	1	0	261	115
1903	James Faragher	8	0	1	292	0	1955	Terry Brennan	8	2	0	210	112
1904	Louis Salmon	5	3	0	94	127	1956	Terry Brennan	2	8	0	130	289
1905	Henry McGlew	5	4	0	312	80	1957	Terry Brennan	7	3	0	200	136
1906	Thomas Barry	6	1	0	107	12	1958	Terry Brennan	6	4	0	206	173
1907	Thomas Barry	6	0	1	137	20	1959	Joe Kuharich	5	5	0	171	180
1908	Harry Miller	8	1	0	326	20	1960	Joe Kuharich	2	8	0	111	188
1909	Howard Edwards	7	0	1	236	14	1961	Joe Kuharich	5	5	0	175	182
1910	Frank Longman	4	1	1	192	25	1962	Joe Kuharich	5	5	0	159	192
1911	John Marks	6	0	2	222	9	1963	Hugh Devore	2	7	0	108	159
1912	John Marks	7	0	0	389	27	1964	Ara Parseghian	9	1	0	287	77
1913	Jesse Harper	7	0	0	268	41	1965	Ara Parseghian	7	2	1	270	73
1914	Jesse Harper	6	2	0	287	61	1966	Ara Parseghian	9	0	1	362	38
1915	Jesse Harper	4	1	1	192	25	1967	Ara Parseghian	8	2	0	337	124
1916	Jesse Harper	8	1	0	293	30	1968	Ara Parseghian	7	2	1	376	170
1917	Jesse Harper	6	1	1	141	9	1969	Ara Parseghian	8	2	1	351	134
1918	Knute Rockne	3	1	2	133	39	1970	Ara Parseghian	10	1	0	354	108
1919	Knute Rockne	9	0	0	229	47	1971	Ara Parseghian	8	2	0	225	86
1920	Knute Rockne	9	0	0	251	41	1972	Ara Parseghian	8	3	0	289	192
1921	Knute Rockne	10	1	0	375	41	1973	Ara Parseghian	11	0	0	382	89
1922	Knute Rockne	8	1	1	222	27	1974	Ara Parseghian	10	2	0	318	147
1923	Knute Rockne	9	1	0	275	37	1975	Dan Devine	8	3	0	244	144
1924	Knute Rockne	10	0	0	285	54	1976	Dan Devine	9	3	0	294	158
1925	Knute Rockne	7	2	1	200	64	1977	Dan Devine	11	1	0	420	139
1926	Knute Rockne	9	1	0	210	38	1978	Dan Devine	9	3	0	293	197
1927	Knute Rockne	7	1	1	158	57	1979	Dan Devine	7	4	0	243	197
1928	Knute Rockne	5	4	0	99	107	1980	Dan Devine	9	2	1	248	128
1929	Knute Rockne	9	0	0	145	38	1981	Gerry Faust	5	6	0	232	160
1930	Knute Rockne	9	0	0	265	74	1982	Gerry Faust	6	4	1	206	174
1931	Hunk Anderson	6	2	1	215	40	1983	Gerry Faust	7	5	0	316	177
1932	Hunk Anderson	7	2	0	255	31	1984	Gerry Faust	7	5	0	299	239
1933	Hunk Anderson	3	5	1	32	80	1985	Gerry Faust	5	6	0	230	234
1934	Elmer Layden	6	3	0	108	56	1986	Lou Holtz	5	6	0	299	219
1935	Elmer Layden	7	1	1	143	62	1987	Lou Holtz	8	4	0	339	218
1936	Elmer Layden	6	2	1	128	69	1988	Lou Holtz	12	0	0	393	156
1937	Elmer Layden	6	2	1	77	49	1989	Lou Holtz	11	1	0	427	189
1938	Elmer Layden	8	1	0	149	39	1990	Lou Holtz	9	3	0	359	259

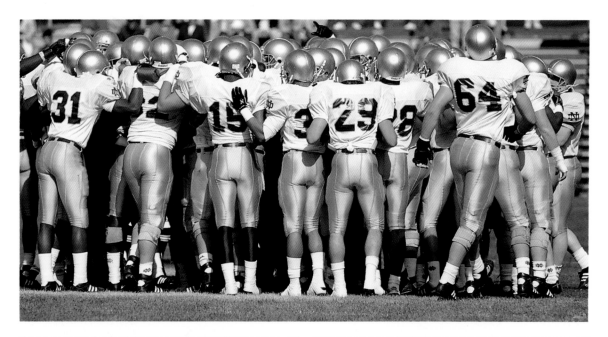

TOP CAREER RUSHERS

	Att	Yds	Avg	TD
1. Allen Pinkett (1982-85)	889	4131	4.6	49
2. Vagas Ferguson (1976-79)	673	3472	5.2	32
3. Jerome Heavens (1975-78)	590	2682	4.5	15
4. Phil Carter (1979-82)	557	2409	4.3	14
5. George Gipp (1917-20)	369	2341	6.3	21

TOP CAREER PASSERS

	Att	Cmp	Yds	TD
1. Steve Beuerlein (1983-86)	850	473	6527	27
2. Terry Hanratty (1966-68)	550	304	4152	27
3. Blair Kiel (1980-83)	609	297	3650	17
4. Joe Theismann (1968-70)	509	290	4411	31
5. Joe Montana (1975-78)	515	268	4121	25

TOP CAREER RECEIVERS

	Yds	Receps	Avg	TD
1. Tom Gatewood (1969-71)	2283	157	14.5	19
2. Jim Seymour (1966-68)	2113	138	15.3	16
3. Tim Brown (1984-87)	2493	137	18.2	12
4. Ken MacAfee (1974-77)	1759	128	13.7	15
5. Tony Hunter (1979-82)	1897	120	15.8	5

TOP CAREER SCORERS

	TD	PAT	FG	Pts
1. Allen Pinkett (1982-85)	53	2	0	320
2. Louis Salmon (1900-03)	36	60	2	250
3. Dave Reeve (1974-77)	0	130	39	247
4. Stan Cofall (1914-16)	30	60	2	246
5. John Carney (1984-86)	0	70	51	223

BOWL RESULTS

The Aloha Bowl – Honolulu, Hawaii
Record: 0-1
1984 – Southern Methodist 27, Notre Dame 20

The Cotton Bowl – Dallas, Texas
Record: 3-2
1970 – Texas 21, Notre Dame 17
1971 – Notre Dame 24, Texas 11
1978 – Notre Dame 38, Texas 10
1979 – Notre Dame 35, Houston 34
1987 – Texas A&M 35, Notre Dame 10

The Fiesta Bowl – Tempe, Arizona
Record: 1-0
1989 – Notre Dame 34, West Virginia 21

The Gator Bowl – Jacksonville, Florida
Record: 1-0
1976 – Notre Dame 20, Penn State 9

The Liberty Bowl – Memphis, Tennessee
Record: 1-0
1983 – Notre Dame 19, Boston College 18

The Orange Bowl – Miami, Florida
Record: 2-1
1973 – Nebraska 40, Notre Dame 6
1975 – Notre Dame 13, Alabama 11
1990 – Notre Dame 21, Colorado 6
1991 – Colorado 10, Notre Dame 9

The Rose Bowl – Pasadena, California
Record: 1-0
1925 – Notre Dame 27, Stanford 10

The Sugar Bowl – New Orleans, Louisiana
Record: 1-1
1973 – Notre Dame 24, Alabama 23
1981 – Georgia 17, Notre Dame 10

Composite Bowl Record: 10-6

Numbers in *italics* indicate illustrations